PR[illegible]
IN [illegible] OPEN AIR

Also available in the "How To Series"

Praying the Lord's Prayer	Terry Virgo
Effective Evangelism	Ben Davies
Growing Up As A Christian	Roger Day
Handling Your Money	John Houghton
Learning To Worship	Phil Rogers
Leading A Housegroup	Richard Haydon-Knowell
Joining The Church	Richard Haydon-Knowell

For further information on the "How To Series" and New Frontiers International, please write to New Frontiers International, 21-23 Clarendon Villas, Hove, Brighton, East Sussex, BN3 3RE.

SERIES EDITOR
TERRY VIRGO

How to...

STUDY SERIES

PRESENTING JESUS IN THE OPEN AIR

MIKE SPRENGER
with Mary Austin

NEW FRONTIERS

WORD PUBLISHING

Word (UK) Ltd
Milton Keynes, England

WORD AUSTRALIA
Heathmont, Victoria, Australia
STRUIK CHRISTIAN BOOKS (PTY) LTD
Salt River, South Africa
ALBY COMMERCIAL ENTERPRISES PTE LTD
Balmoral Road, Singapore
CONCORDE DISTRIBUTORS LTD
Havelock North, New Zealand
CROSS (HK) CO
Hong Kong

PRESENTING JESUS IN THE OPEN AIR

Published by Word (UK) Ltd/New Frontiers.

ISBN 0–85009–181–6 (Australia 1–86258052–9)

Typeset by Suripace, Milton Keynes and printed and bound in Great Britain by Cox & Wyman Ltd., Reading.

INTRODUCTION

The 'How to' series has been published with a definite purpose in view. It provides a set of workbooks suitable either for housegroups or individuals who want to study a particular Bible theme in a practical way. The goal is not simply to look up verses and fill in blank spaces on the page, but to fill in gaps in our lives and so increase our fruitfulness and our knowledge of God.

Peter wrote his letters to 'stimulate wholesome thinking' (2 Peter 3:1). He required his readers to think as well as read! We hope the training manual approach of this book will have the same effect. *Stop, think, apply* and *act* are key words.

If you are using the book on your own, we suggest you work through the chapters systematically, Bible at your side and pen in hand. If you are doing it as a group activity, it is probably best to do all the initial reading and task work before the group sessions - this gives more time for discussion on key issues which may be raised.

All quotations from the Bible are from the New International Version, which the reader is expected to use in filling in the study material.

Terry Virgo
Series Editor

NEW FRONTIERS INTERNATIONAL is a team ministry led by Terry Virgo and involved in planting and equipping churches according to New Testament principles with a view to reaching this generation with the gospel of the Kingdom. They are also responsible for a wide range of conferences, training programmes and the production of printed and audio teaching materials.

Contents

Chapter One
JESUS IN THE OPEN AIR

Revival - the heartcry of the people of God! An 'ordinary' Christian life of churchgoing and good deeds no longer satisfies or excites us. We sense a call into something greater. The Spirit is urging us to acknowledge that our God is not only able to save but to perform signs and wonders as well. Indifference is being replaced by zeal. We are beginning to expect God to use us in powerful ways and to make His name great in our time.

This book has been written with the conviction that revival will surely come to this nation. It was also written in full assurance that God wants to involve His people in His plans. John the Baptist was called from birth to prepare people for the coming of Jesus. We are commissioned from rebirth to be co-workers with God in establishing His Kingdom until Jesus returns.

Fill in the missing words in these verses then check your answer in Matthew 28: 18-20.

'All authority in heaven and on earth ....

to me. Therefore .... and .... disciples

of all nations, ... them in the name of the Father and

of the Son and of the Holy Spirit, and .... them to ....

everything I .... you.'

The average unbeliever is indifferent to God. The Lord is not relevant to him. Jesus is a swear word, not a living person, and Christianity is a religion not a supernatural lifestyle. Every believer knows that the world's greatest need is for a Saviour from sin and he also knows who that Saviour is. Jesus does not expect us to hide the best news that the world will ever hear. He trusts us to share it.

Rearrange the following into a Biblical verse:

Believe can have heard how in not of one the they they whom?

....

Can and hear how preaching someone them they to without?

....

Check your answer in Romans 10:14.

Jesus said, 'You will be my witnesses' (Acts 1:8). If we are determined to see God at work in our nation, each of us must be willing to be used. Prayer and talk about evangelism will not reach people with the gospel and neither will leaving the outreach to everyone else. God wants us on our knees asking to be filled with His Spirit, and on our feet boldly sharing the good news. We need to have a well-planned strategy and a tried and tested means of fulfilling it.

1. STRATEGIES

Jesus had a strategy for reaching people with His message. He began in the small villages and worked His way towards Jerusalem. One moment He was talking to Nicodemus away from the crowds (John 3:1-21), the next He was teaching and feeding over five thousand people in the open air (John 6:1-15). A quiet, personal witness to individuals went hand in hand with a very public ministry to the masses.

Write down other examples of Jesus' contact with:

Individuals or small groups

(i) ....

(ii) ....

(iii) ....

(Clue: try Mark 5:22, 23, 35-43).

Large crowds

(i) ....

(ii) ....

(iii) ....
(Clue: try Luke 14: 25-35).

Like Jesus, the apostle Paul had a strategy for reaching people with the gospel message. He went first of all to the Jews and then to the Gentiles and spoke with individuals and preached to large crowds. Whenever he had the chance to share the good news, he would do so. Consumed by his mission, he declared, 'I have become all things to all men so that by all possible means I might save some' (1 Cor. 9:22).

In essence, there is a twofold means of sharing the gospel:

a) By 'Personal' Means

Every Christian should be involved in sharing the gospel in a personal way. Not only should we be ready to witness at school, college or work, we should also consider becoming badminton players, cake-makers, cinema-goers and football enthusiasts. Our goal is to create the contacts with unbelievers so that we can talk to them about Jesus.

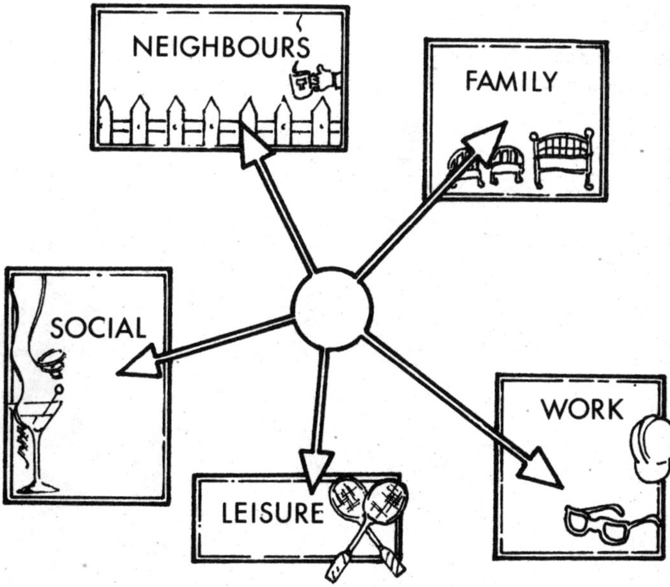

How could you get involved with more non-Christians? (e.g. play tennis with friends, adult education course)

....

....

b) By 'Public' Means

Some of us prefer to think that the public proclamation of the gospel is for others to do. We are happy to build up contacts with our neighbours and friends, but are reluctant to plunge into schools work, door-to-doors and open airs ourselves. We would prefer to witness 'on the quiet'; what we actually mean quite often is that we are too frightened to be involved in a more public way!

When we look at the Scriptures, however, we realise that neither Jesus nor the New Testament disciples relied solely on 'personal' ways of presenting the gospel to the world. Alongside an underlying evangelistic lifestyle ran a far more dynamic and public ministry. Peter got up on the day of Pentecost and three thousand were saved (Acts 2:14-41). If he had relied on 'personal' evangelism, he would have spent a very long time talking to everyone and encouraging them to put their trust in the Lord!

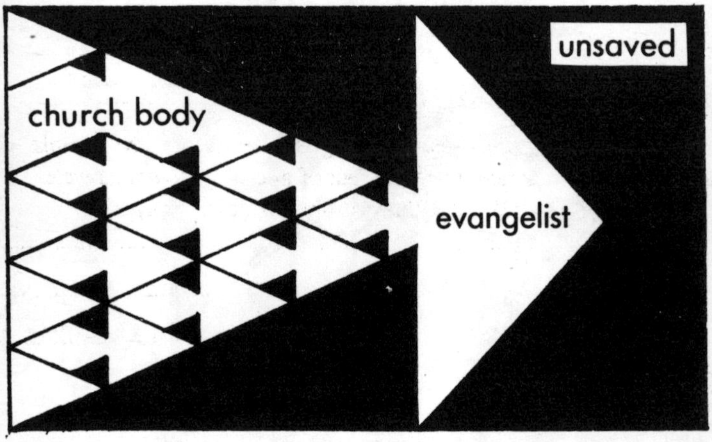

If the evangelists in a church equip the members to engage in evangelism those members will be able to reach out and become involved themselves.

Read Acts 1:8. Where does the power to witness come from?

....

Spend three minutes praying for greater power to witness.

2. OPEN AIRS

Open air evangelism is no new idea. It played a major part in the life of the New Testament Church.

Where did the following evangelistic activities take place and what were the results?

	Location	Result
Luke 19:1-10	....	....
		....
John 4:4-30	....	....
		....
John 7:28-31	....	....
		....
Acts 16:13-15	....	....
		....

When the disciples shared the gospel publicly, the people were aware not just of a new teaching, but of a mighty power as well.

Look up Acts 4:29-30. What was the disciples' prayer?

....

....

Now read Acts 5:12-16 and 8:5-8. What was the result of that prayer?

....

....

Surely, if God added hundreds to the Church and performed amazing miracles in New Testament streets, He can do the same in ours. What a prospect! Imagine the impact of a spectacular open air demonstration of God's healing power on the Saturday shoppers in your town! If God's Church is glorious, shouldn't we be making that glory visible to everyone? Open air evangelism is probably the most effective means we have of presenting the gospel to the general public.

a) Benefits

An open air:

(i) reaches people who have no contact with Christianity or church members.

(ii) enables the Church to reach large numbers effectively. (It is not unrealistic to expect five hundred people to see or hear something about Jesus - even if it's only a banner - at an average Saturday open air.)

(iii) elevates the profile of Jesus and His Church in the community at large in a way that 'personal' evangelism never can.

(iv) breaks down stereotypes of what Christianity is all about. Joy, laughter, colour, dancing and confidence are all things which many non-Christians may never associate with Jesus' Church.

(v) provides a focal point for 'friendly' conversations e.g. 'Was that your lot I saw in town on Saturday?'

(vi) provides countless opportunities for Christians to gain valuable experience in one-to-one conversations, public speaking and praying for the sick.

Write down any more benefits of open air evangelism that may occur to you.

....

....

....

If there are so many advantages to open air evangelism, it's surprising that many of us have never really taken it seriously. Even the great open air preacher John Wesley was, at first, very reluctant to preach outdoors - as his journal indicates:

> It was on the 2nd April, 1739, from a small rise that at four in the afternoon I submitted to be more vile (rather than preach in a church building) and proclaimed in the highways the glad tidings of salvation.

Yet Wesley later became known more for his outdoor ministry than for his indoor one. His father had evidently sown the seed and John was privileged to see the fruit, as his journal again reveals:

> Sunday 13th June, 1742 - At six I preached for the last time in Epworth Church yard to a vast multitude gathered together from all parts. I continued among them for near three hours; and yet we scarce knew how to part. Oh let none think his labour of love is lost because the fruit does not immediately appear! Near forty years did my father labour here, but he saw little fruit of all his labour. I took some pains among this people too, and my strength also seemed spent in vain; but now the fruit appeared.

> Monday 27th April, 1761 - I preached at eight in the market-place at Wigton. The congregation, when I began, consisted of one woman, two boys, and three or four little girls, but in a quarter of an hour we had most of the town.

Wesley did not concern himself with the fact that his father had preached without much success. Neither did he worry over the initial size of the crowds. His desire was rather to be faithful to God and to allow Him to manifest Himself in whatever way He chose.

Read Luke 16:10. How could this verse relate to open air evangelism?

....

....

b) Involvement

Jesus, the early disciples, George Whitefield, John Wesley, Billy

Graham and countless others all bear witness that open air evangelism should be a vital part of our involvement in the Kingdom of God. This does not mean that every church member must stand up and preach, but it does suggest that the entire fellowship should be committed to establishing a more visible demonstration of the Church to the world.

We are living in exciting times. Christianity is at last being seen as something far more dynamic than 'pew-filling and lending a hand to the needy'. It is a high-quality way of life which encompasses a whole supernatural dimension. Such good news cannot be allowed to lie dormant within us or to remain confined in our fellowship meeting places. We dare not just wait for people to come to us before they ever hear the gospel. The command from Jesus to his followers was not 'sit and wait' but 'go and make' (Matthew 28:19)!

How did they respond and what happened?

....

.... (Mark 16:20)

What is your opinion now about open air evangelism?

....

....

Give reasons for your answer.

....

....

Chapter 2
STARTING OUT

When Jesus returned to heaven He left his followers with one great commission, 'Go and make disciples ...' (Matthew 28:19). He had already taught them many principles of ministry (Matthew 10; Luke 10) but He left them responsible for implementing the practical details. Using the same underlying principles, we need to communicate the same basic gospel truths in a creative way.

Thus, in an age where we are competing with a vast number of alternative attractions, an impressive visual display will halt the passer-by in his tracks and encourage him to listen to the gospel.
Make a list of words which, for you, describe an open air.

Singing, joy, ...

....

....

....

....

A group doing this exercise came up with eighty six words which ranged from 'colour' to 'clarity' and 'preaching' to 'pigeons'!

Although God wants us to put our individual mark on how we run our open air, there are some general principles we shall need to follow. These will make a significant difference to the success or failure of our outreach.

1. WHAT ABOUT LOCATION?

We have already looked at some New Testament examples of open air evangelism. Now read the following passages, note the location of each event and suggest a possible modern day equivalent.

	New Testament Location	**Modern Equivalent**
John 4:4-6	Jacob's Well	Pub Garden
Mark 1:33	....	....
Luke 5:1-3	....	....
Acts 2:5-15	....	....
Acts 3:11	....	....
Acts 16:13	....	....
Acts 17:17	....	....

I have participated in open airs in all of the following locations: in a shopping centre, on a main road, outside a railway station, in a pedestrian precinct, on a university campus, in a park, on a beach, at a village square/green, in a children's playground, near a football ground, outside a pub, in a market, outside school gates and in a car park. The list is endless.

Now consider your own city/town/village and list three possible open air locations.

1...

2. ....

3. ....

Which is the best day of the week and time of day for each of these?

	Day:	**Time:**
1.	....	....
2.	....	....
3.	....	....

2. WHAT ABOUT LEADERSHIP?

The risk of disorganisation is considerably minimised if all decisions are channelled through one named individual. It is his or her job to oversee everything that goes on and will, in practical terms, involve:

a) Delegating responsibility

Who will make the banners? Who will sing or play, act or speak? Who does what and when must be decided in advance and written down. The leader must communicate to everyone exactly what is expected of him/her.

b) Checking that things are happening

Well before the open air, the leader must know if the groundwork is being done. Incomplete banners, unlearned songs, poorly-rehearsed drama and last-minute speaking preparation will do little for the advance of the Kingdom of God! We should communicate excellence. It is the leader's responsibility to keep the standard high.

c) Taking 'on the street' decisions

Unforeseen last-minute decisions will doubtless need to be made. Committee-style conferences on the pavement will lead to a lack of confidence in the group and are likely to confuse onlookers, conveying uncertainty to them. Clearly the leader must be someone who not only prepares the way beforehand but who actually turns up to direct on the day.

What sort of unforeseen difficulties might a leader encounter? (e.g. buskers on your chosen site).

....

....

....

d) Following up

Immediately after the open air, (while the group is still together on the street), the leader should bring everyone together to review briefly what has been happening. What went well and were there any good contacts with people? The open air should be concluded as it began - with a short time of prayer.

3. WHAT ABOUT VISUAL IMPACT?

If you want to make an impact on people, do not turn up to an open air looking as though you have been sleeping in your old painting gear and have just rolled out of bed! Wear colourful clothes and look happy. No one else has a more exciting message to share with the world than you. Your joy should puzzle the average passer-by and make him wonder what on earth you have got to be so enthusiastic about.

Make your banner(s) big and bright. They can be made quite simply from sheets, remnants of material and spray paint. A large, colourful, intelligently-placed banner will catch the attention of passer-by and motorist alike. In some ways, it won't matter if the depressed individual on the top of the number 85 bus never hears a word you say. He may be provoked by the banner which states boldly: 'Jesus loves you'.

Sketch some of your Ideas here

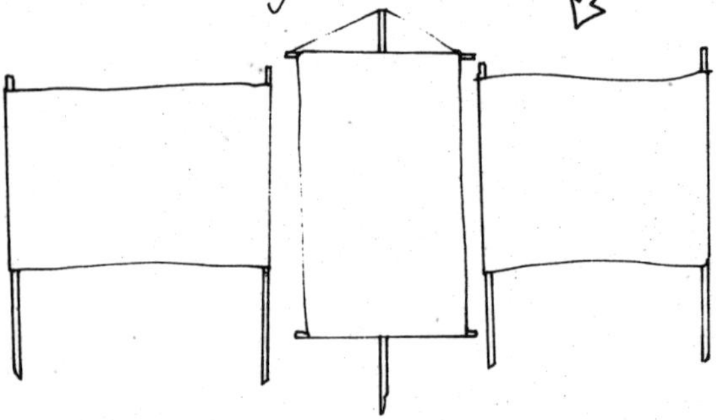

4. WHAT ABOUT THE PARTICIPANTS?

Every Christian can be involved in an open air in one of the following four way:

a) The 'Rent a Crowd'

There are bound to be members in your church who do not wish to take an 'up front' role in the open air. Far from being redundant, they are crucial 'crowd draw-ers' - particularly if they stand around watching as the event starts. At the end they can turn to those who have been watching and engage them in conversation.

b) Semi-involved Group Members

Not all the group members are likely to be participating all the time. Those not involved in say, the drama, should resist the temptation to go 'off duty', hide themselves away and chat to their Christian friends. Rather, they should join whatever crowd there is and swell the number of onlookers as much as possible.

c) Literature Distributors

About thirty metres away from the crowd several individuals should be handing out literature to the people who walk past but who don't stop. They should also be seeking to talk to those who watch for a while and then move on.

d) Core Group Members

Group positioning is important. A long line of singers is not good either visually or vocally. A tight bunch of people with instruments at either end will create a far better effect.

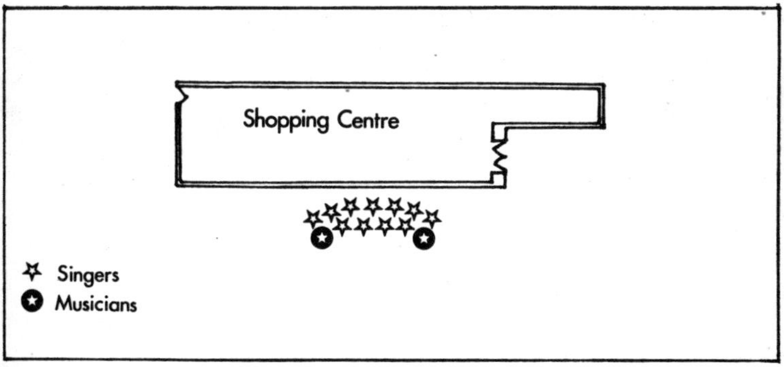

Remember, your message has to compete with many other pressing issues in the minds of your hearers. If you delay too long between items, your audience will depart. The secret lies in good planning and good leadership.

5. WHAT ABOUT PROBLEMS?

Our enemy, the devil, is scared of open airs. If he can unnerve you by suggesting that there will be all sorts of problems (rather than challenges) you may not want to get started. Let's identify some of these challenges.

a) Gulp - there's a police car over there!

Under English Common Law we are guaranteed freedom of speech and assembly in a public place. This includes all streets, pavements and most shopping centres. So an individual can, at any time, stand on a street corner and say whatever he wants (subject, of course, to other laws affecting trading, drunkenness, obscenity and treason!) Unless your chosen spot is a privately-owned shopping centre, you are not required to ask permission to hold an open air, or inform the police about it. You can simply go ahead.

The only difficulty you may come up against relates to the poorly-defined law concerning 'obstruction'. Technically, if you are standing looking into a shop window you are obstructing someone else's right to pass by on that particular space of pavement. In practice, of course, the police virtually never take any action unless the blockage is quite serious. So you may be asked to move on if people are having to step out into the road to avoid you or the crowd that is watching you. If this does happen, don't complain, just find a better site somewhere else.

Although you do not need to ask for permission to hold an open air, it is considerate to inform shop/pub owners before standing in front of their premises. It is helpful if you avoid causing an obstruction or blocking a window display.

b) Did you feel that spot of rain?

Don't just hope that the weather will be all right on the day, plan in advance what you are going to do if it isn't. Then, if it rains, you can continue your open air under cover. If it is severely cold the best solution is to make the whole event brisk and musical and to focus on literature distribution. Above all, be realistic. No one is going to stand listening to you for twenty minutes as a snowdrift builds up around his legs! Abandon the event!

c) That mn over there is just about to disagree with you

You can expect people to pass by and joke about your preaching to the friends who are with them. They do not, however, present as much of a problem as those who want to stand and argue. Hecklers do not often turn up but when they do, they tend to fall into one or more of the following categories: humourous, drunk, political or religious. If you are shouted at, remember that the crowd will usually be on your side. Do not insult the heckler back or the crowd will turn against you. Try instead to ignore him and simply carry on. If it's possible, someone should lead him away from the rest of the group and talk quietly to him. What's his name? Where's he from? Be genuinely interested and seek to calm the situation rather than stir it up.

Leader's Checklist
1. Establish the location, date and time of the open air and ensure that everyone knows about it.
2. Find an alternative wet weather location (i.e. in an arcade, under a bridge).
3. Outline the content of the open air and allocate people to the various tasks.
4. List everything you plan to take with you and delegate someone to see it all arrives.
5. Invite the church and ask for prayer support.
6. Check to see that the groundwork is being done (i.e. rehearsals, preaching preparation, screen-making etc).
7. Tell everyone the order of events and who's doing what.
8. Arrange for everyone to meet beforehand for praise and prayer.
9. Start on time.
10. Keep it short and punchy.
11. Collect details of interested onlookers.
12. Hold a feedback and evaluation session.
13. Ask someone to give a three minute report at the next church prayer meeting. Those who attended should be encouraged and those who did not should be warmly invited to do so next time.

Can you think of anything else a leader should do?

....

....

....

....

Chapter Three
CHOICES

You do not need a screwdriver to change a plug. You can use a kitchen knife. A screwdriver, however, tends to be a more effective instrument than a knife for plug-changing because it was made for that sort of job. If you plan to preserve your plug screws, you will not leave it long before you get hold of a screwdriver. If possible, it's always best to use the right tool for any task.

An open air should be tailor-made for the job in hand. In other words, it's best not to busk where there are too many other attractions to catch the attention of the passer-by. It's not a good idea to press on with a complex programme when there's a sudden snowstorm! And if you plan to have about fifty singers, make sure there are more instruments than one guitar to accompany them! Since God is sovereign, He will certainly work through an open air which is not really appropriate for the group/onlookers. But isn't it better to try to get the maximum effect by applying the most suitable open air to the situation right from the start?

1. DIFFERENT OPEN AIRS

In essence, there are four types of open air:

a) Creative

b) Congregational

c) Casual

d) Carnival

Once you have decided which of them is most appropriate to your circumstances, you can adapt it to suit your own requirements. Never feel that you have to stick rigidly to the format of any of the models.

There is no 'correct method' of doing an open air. These suggested types should be viewed as guidelines, not unchangeable structures. They are designed to inspire your thinking, not to restrict it.

a) A 'Creative' Open Air

The keyword to this form of open air is 'variety'. The programme includes three or four songs, testimony, drama and preaching. Individuals hand out leaflets and seek to engage onlookers in conversation. By dramatising or preaching on various social problems, the group reaches out to people where they hurt. It is therefore a very 'specific' means of communicating the gospel which can be extremely effective if you know what needs there are in your neighbourhood.

List the particular social needs in your community (e.g. high unemployment, poverty, racial tension.)

....

....

....

....

In practice:

Take, say, thirty individuals. They have been practising for their 'creative' open air and have just met to pray for the last time about it. They pile into cars and congregate at the town centre shopping precinct. The leader divides them into two groups: twenty who are involved in playing instruments, singing (and later, perhaps, drama and preaching) and ten who will distribute literature and talk to the onlookers.

Two of the tallest singers stand at the back and hold a banner which declares, 'New Life in Jesus' or something similar. The rest of the singers stand in one close group in front of the banner. The musicians stand at either end and face inwards. All twenty then sing three or four lively songs. Immediately after the last song, one of the singers talks for three or four minutes about how he/she came to know Jesus. The same person then introduces the drama.

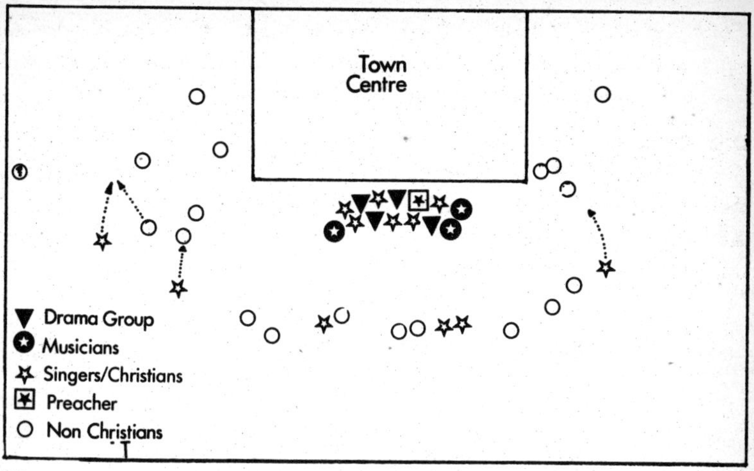

The actors step forward and everyone else disperses and forms a crowd around the drama. The preacher links his message with the drama and speaks for about seven minutes. He concludes by saying something like, 'If this has interested you, please talk to one of the Christians in the crowd'. The meeting has lasted about twenty minutes

While the open air has been going on, the ten literature distributors have been handing out leaflets and engaging people in conversation or in questionnaires. Now that the meeting is over, they are joined by the singers, actors and speakers who themselves become involved in one-to-one witnessing. When all the individual conversations have finished, the whole open air can be repeated on the same spot or at a different location.

b) A 'Congregational' Open Air

There are churches where most of the members have never testified about Jesus to lots of people. It may be too nerve-racking for them to plunge into a 'creative' open air at first. They will need to build up confidence. One answer is to hold a 'congregational' meeting which will involve singing, leaflet distribution and one-to-one witnessing.

In practice:

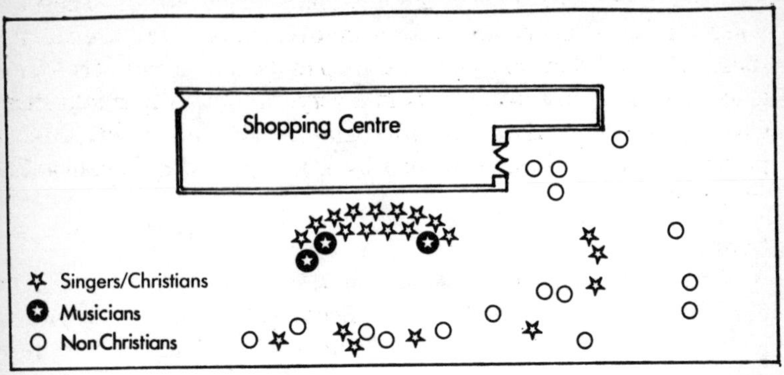

The church gathers in the shopping centre on a Saturday afternoon. Ten of them stand on the edge of the open air ready to hand out literature, chat to people and give balloons to the children. The message on each balloon is the same as the one on the banner held by two at the back of the singing group. It reads something like, 'Jesus brings freedom and life'.

Do some research and come up with a balloon supplier who will print a slogan on your balloons.

Name: ....

Address:...

Phone No: ....

One of the musicians is in overall control of the group who form rows in a semi-circle. Those with instruments stand at either end. The musicians then lead everyone in twenty to thirty minutes of lively worship. When the group disperses, its individual members can join the leaflet/balloon distributors and talk to anyone who looks interested.

After a church has held a couple of 'congregational' open airs it should begin to consider holding a 'creative' one. Maybe some adventurous members could even launch out as buskers.

c) A 'Casual' Open Air

Casual open airs are not sloppy, unrehearsed events. They are simply relaxed occasions which involve only a few musicians (buskers). What they do is very much up to them to decide. Their goal is to come alongside unbelievers in a very informal way and to share Christ with them. Even an individual busker can be effective - particularly if he is accompanied by a group of people-contacting supporters.

In practice:

A band of about four individuals practise together for a couple of months. They then find four other church members who are willing to witness to onlookers and distribute literature or conduct questionnaires.

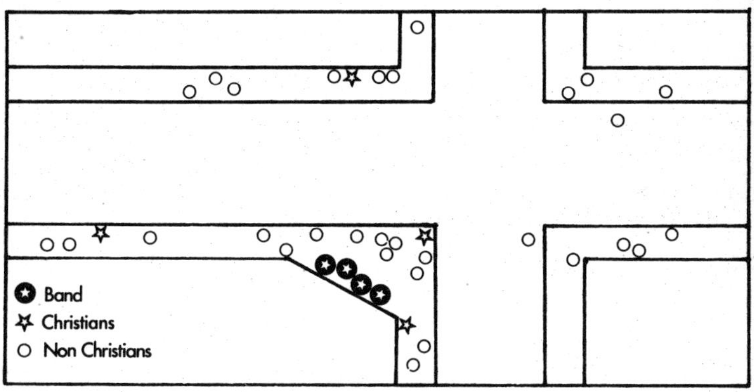

The group stand on a wide but busy pavement on a street corner. They are away from traffic and not directly outside any shop doorway. While they are singing, their friends mingle with the crowd, give out literature/complete questionnaires and chat to people. After about five songs, one of the group members preaches for about five minutes and concludes by inviting the passers-by to a guest service the following Sunday. No one receives any money.

There are several advantages to this form of evangelism:

a) Flexibility - it does not require a programme and can include testimonies and purely instrumental songs.

b) Informality - it encourages a relaxed atmosphere.

c) Universality - it can be done almost anywhere.

Remember that with busking, the music's primary function is to be a focal point for the purpose of engaging in one-to-one conversations. For this reason some church members may need experience in personal evangelism before they are confident enough to be involved.

Another informal way of reaching the general public is for three or four individuals to go onto the street and take it in turns to preach the gospel to people. While one is speaking, the others hand out literature to the passers-by and, when appropriate, engage them in conversation.

This approach can be particularly effective where there is a static audience - people sitting having lunch in a precinct or park.

d) A 'Carnival' Open Air (covered in detail in chapters 9 and 10)

Large open air events declare Jesus to big crowds. They include praise marches, children's fundays, town festivals and celebration events. If you know that people will be gathering for something, don't miss the opportunity to be there with them!

2. WHICH OPEN AIR TO CHOOSE

The sort of open air a church chooses will depend on its abilities and location. It would be encouraging to see every church involved in all four types of meeting - and any others with which they might experiment.

Bearing in mind what you have read about the four basic open air models, decide which one would probably be most appropriate for the following churches. Give reasons for your answer.

(i) A small church with a few talented musicians

Type: ....

Reason: ....

....

(ii) A small, very active church keen to have a big impact on a small town

Type: ....

Reason: ....

....

(iii) A large church with little experience in evangelism

Type: ....

Reason: ....

....

(iv) A church with an effective drama group and several capable musicians

Type: ....

Reason: ....

....

Now decide which type of open air would be appropriate for the following venues. Again, give reasons for your choice.

(i) Outside a railway station at 8.00 a.m. or 5.30 p.m.

Type: ....

Reason: ....

(ii) In a partially-covered shopping precinct in a large town

Type: ....

Reason: ....

(iii) On a corner of a field at the Town Fete

Type: ....

Reason: ....

(iv) On a busy and noisy high street on a Saturday morning

Type: ....

Reason: ....

What sort of open air would you like to be involved in?

....

What would you do in it?

....

Expect to see God at work whenever you go out. Many will take a leaflet and some will stop to talk. If you ask, most will let you pray with them. Love the people and you will win them - wherever you go, whatever type of open air you adopt. In the final analysis it's the reality of Jesus in you that will touch people's hearts.

Chapter Four
MUSIC

Ingredients are as important to an open air as they are to a cake. Once you have chosen what sort of open air you want to conduct, you will need to be specific about what you want to do in it.

Music has always played an important role in revival and it is one of the most vital elements in an open air. It is an effective means of communicating Biblical truths and provides an excellent platform for preaching.

The Scriptures contain many examples of the importance of music and singing in the lives of God's people.

Read Nehemiah 12:43. Where could the rejoicing be heard?

....

Sometimes God chose to deliver His people through their worship rather than their swords.

Read 2 Chronicles 20:21,22. Where were the musicians placed?

....

What happened as they began to sing and praise?

....

Israel's faith here lay not in their worship but in their God. All praise is a weapon against the enemy but God does not necessarily deliver us in the way we expect. Daniel escaped the lions' mouths, but the majority of the early Christians died in the arena, even though they had songs of joy and victory on their lips.

MUSIC IN THE OPEN AIR

Our joy at being Christians should spill over to the unsaved. The psalmist declares:

'May ....
joy.' (Psalm 67:4)

When we begin an open air with music, we are actually doing four things:

a) delighting in God;

b) declaring to the world His victory over the enemy;

c) demonstrating that our joy is far superior to the world's;

d) drawing people's interest in who we are and what we are doing.

Music is something in which almost everyone in the church can take part. A joyful group singing and playing contemporary songs will immediately demand the attention and feed the curiosity of the public. 'What's going on over there?' they will ask themselves and move closer to listen. Our songs are geared to tell them, in a lively and attractive way, who God is and what He's done for us. Moses and Miriam did this before the Israelites (Ex 15:1- 21). We must not underestimate the power of the 'musical Word'. A well-chosen and well-sung song may easily communicate profound Scriptural truth and cause people to stop and watch the rest of the open air.

1. CONCERNING SONGS

There is no shortage of Christian songs. They combine to exalt every aspect of God's character and works: His majesty, power, faithfulness, love, fatherhood, wonders, patience, promises - to name but a few. There are also songs which declare God's Kingdom on earth. Many songs have a simple melody line and can be sung in unison by any number of people. Others are more complex and could be 'performed' by a small group. Above all else the songs we choose must relate to those who will be listening. This means:

a) No Jargon

We may rejoice that we have been clothed in righteousness, washed in the blood of the Lamb and seated with Him in heavenly places. The general public, however, will notice that we actually look like very ordinary human beings. We may not be able completely to avoid jargon, but we can keep it to a minimum.

b) No Hymns

To say that we must never sing hymns may be going too far. God could mightily use a moving rendering of *When I survey* and we need to allow for that. In the main, however, it is wiser to avoid hymns. They do not relate well to the average man in the street and the verses are generally difficult to remember.

If our songs relate to our time, they must also communicate to the individual. This means:

(i) Choose Short Songs

If we select a long chorus, the chances are that we shall forget which verse follows which. Our hesitation will cause our voices to drop and that, in turn, will communicate uncertainty to the public. The simple answer is to concentrate on short songs.

(ii) Learn the Songs

When people know what they are singing, the words come across much more powerfully than when they don't. We want our message to travel up the street as far as possible, so we can't afford to be riveted to bits of paper. If we learn the words, we shall be able to look at the public and present the good news to them rather than down to our feet.

(iii) Sing clearly

Mumbled words do not express truth well! In a noisy shopping precinct we shall need to pronounce our words distinctly if we want them to be understood. Let's not allow our nervousness to remove the cutting edge from our message. It's a good idea to ask someone to stand a hundred metres from our next open air and report back afterwards on how much came across.

(iv) Try a Little Variety

- Try writing your own songs.
- Run two or more songs together.

Find a songbook and list ten songs which you feel would be suitable for an open air. (Graham Kendrick and Dave Fellingham albums may give you some ideas.)

1.	6. ....
2.	7. ....
3.	8. ....
4.	9. ....
5.	10. ....

2. CONCERNING INSTRUMENTS

Guitars lead singing best but they can be backed up well by almost any other portable instrument. Is there anyone in your church who plays the saxophone, clarinet or trumpet? Now is the time to find out. Remember that the instruments you choose will influence your performance for better or worse. Some instruments sound better together than others. And it might not be a good idea to have a band of nine enthusiastic instrumentalists accompanying a group of five singers.

* * * *

Tips

a) Before the open air begins make sure that the instruments are in tune with each other.

b) Try including a few interesting percussion instruments (e.g. cowbells, maracas) to add flavour to some lively tunes.

c) Do not use P.A. equipment or you may find yourselves contravening certain bye-laws. In any event, the presence of loudspeakers often creates an unhealthy 'them and us' situation.

d) Music stands get in the way and are prone to falling over in windy conditions so do not use them. Memorize the chords instead.

e) A 'song order' list should be available to all musicians. Try blu-tacking it to your instrument.

f) Guitarists should carry spare strings or even a spare (tuned) guitar. If you snap a string, wait for a convenient break before doing anything about it.

g) Fingerless gloves were obviously invented with musicians in mind! If it gets too cold, just press on regardless!

h) As far as possible the programme should be arranged so that musicians do not have to preach or act directly after playing.

* * * *

List the members of your church who can play an appropriate instrument well.

1. .... 4. ....

2. .... 5. ....

3. .... 6. ....

3. CONCERNING DANCING

King David had no hang-ups about leaping and dancing before the Lord in public. Rather, he thoroughly enjoyed himself! (2 Samuel 6:14). Much to the amusement of all who watched, an evangelistic team once did a conga around the local shopping precinct! Such behaviour certainly gives the church a new and lively image.
List some songs you could dance to.

1. .... 4. ....

2. .... 5. ....

3. .... 6. ....

BRINGING IT ALL TOGETHER

Music in an open air meeting doesn't just happen! It has to be organised. The group will need someone to look to for guidance in the worship. This person is normally one of the guitarists.

In planning the worship, the leader and his assistant will need to consider:

a) The audience — What sort of people will be watching?

b) The group — Is it a good location? Will sound projection be effective? if a crowd forms, will there be

	enough space for people to pass? Who will stand where? (taller people at the back, shorter at the front, instruments at either end where both the audience and singers can hear them).
c) The songs	Which songs are most suitable for the audience?
d) The rehearsal	Do people know what they are doing? Are the beginnings and endings of the songs tidy?

Before the open air begins, the worship leader should run through a list of the songs to remind everyone which song follows which. The group should then be reminded to relax, pronounce words clearly and look as if they are enjoying themselves - which, we hope, they will be!

Work out a possible musical programme for your next open air.

Leader: ....

His/Her Assistant: ....

Songs (all together): ....

....

....

....

Songs (solo/small group): ....

....

Instruments: Played by:

....

....

....

The rehearsal will be on: .... at ....

Have fun!

Chapter Five
DRAMA

When Jesus addressed the crowds, 'He did not say anything to them without using a parable' (Matt 13:14). Clearly He understood that the best way to communicate the truth was to use stories that people could imagine. God had spoken in a similar way before.
Write down the name and vision/dream of:

	Name	Vision/Dream
a) an Old Testament character	....	....
b) an Old Testament prophet	....	....
c) a New Testament character	....	....
d) someone in your church	....	....

God did not speak to His people through mental pictures alone. He added another dimension and chose individuals to dramatise His Word in public.
Read Ezekiel 12:3-6 and list the specific actions that the prophet was told to do.

(i) .... (v 3)

(ii) .... (v 4a)

(iii) .... (v 4b)

(iv) .... (v 5)

(v) .... (v 6a)

(vi) .... (v 6b)

What theme was the prophet seeking to communicate through this acted out parable?

....

....

Briefly describe the drama that Jeremiah is told to enact (Jer 19:1-2; 10-11)

....

....

....

What is God saying to Judah through the drama?

....

.... (v.11)

POWER BEHIND DRAMA

Well-written and acted drama is an exceptionally powerful means of communication.

a) It appeals to all ages and backgrounds.

b) It counteracts people's stereotypes of Church and Christianity.

c) It leaves people with pictures which will stick in their minds.

d) It can confront and address human ills and relate to people's inner feelings e.g. family breakdown, fear, pride and so on.

e) It can emphasise a single doctrinal point, for example the incarnation, the cross or man's sin.

f) Several sketches run together will often stop a large crowd.

Who knows what God may do through your open air drama? One day you may learn about someone who became a Christian after being challenged by what you did in your high street presentation a few days, weeks or even years before. There could be no greater motivation than that.

STARTING OUT

1. Preparation

a) Commitment

Under the word 'commitment' in one dictionary are these words: 'an obligation, promise etc. that restricts freedom of action'. There's a sense in which the whole open air needs the commitment of the group concerned. Drama, however, requires a high level of it. That's because acting involves interaction between individuals. They must spend time together.

The ideal drama leader has had some previous acting experience but the absence of such a person should not deter you from launching out in drama. Commitment for the leader will mean organising prayer times and regular rehearsals (probably in a large room or church hall). It will also mean taking responsibility for seeing the project through from beginning to end.

On the actors' part, commitment will mean attending prayer times and rehearsals (if only on a short term basis). It will mean being teachable and not rude or silly. It will mean not pulling out when the excitement is no longer evident and when lines and actions have got to be learnt.

If you gather a group of committed people together, God will do great things through them.

b) Rehearsals

When the drama group begins rehearsing, the actors should concentrate on warming up before they try specific sketches. Play a few games and go on to improvisation (creating a drama without a script). Each member should act out a character or situation from everyday life. Characters and situations can later be swapped around among group members.

Add your ideas to these characters and situations:

Character	**Situation**
army officer	sitting in a dentist's chair
film star	waiting for a bus
punk rocker	attending a funeral
....	....
....	....
....	....
....	....
....	....

Many other useful warm-up games and techniques can be found in *In Drama*, one of Scripture Union's *Using the Bible* series.

Once you have 'loosened up' you can begin learning some actual plays. The 'Box Sketch' is simple and effective. It is included at the end of this chapter as something you can use immediately. It may also stimulate you to write your own material.

If a group is committed to working hard, (corporately and individually) the results will be good. Early on in the rehearsals discuss among yourselves how the drama could be improved. About two weeks before the open air, you should have any major alterations nailed down. After this time, any further changes may confuse the cast who might, in their 'performance day nervousness' forget which change was in force. Practice projecting your voices - they are easily lost in the open air. This is why most sketches leave the dialogue to a narrator or one or two main characters, while the others provide action and interest.

A dress rehearsal is essential. It should be the final and complete run-through and must include all the actors, all the costumes and all the props. By this time, the leader should have ensured that the words and actions are virtually perfect. All he or she should have to do is correct a few weak areas and offer encouragement for the forthcoming event.

2. Props

The more visually striking the props are, the greater the interest in the drama will be. Characters may be identified simply by headgear: top hat, crash helmet, school cap, beret, chef's hat and so on, or by a whole outfit. If the whole group dresses in a similar style or colour(s), it gives cohesion and sets you apart from the crowd. Avoid just wearing jeans and pullovers unless you are playing a particular character who needs them.

Screens are cheap, lightweight and fairly simple to construct. They provide either a focal point for drama or can act as a backdrop to the whole open air meeting. Card or canvas can easily be attached to the wooden frame to create a variety of backgrounds. Additional supports at the base may be required in windy locations.

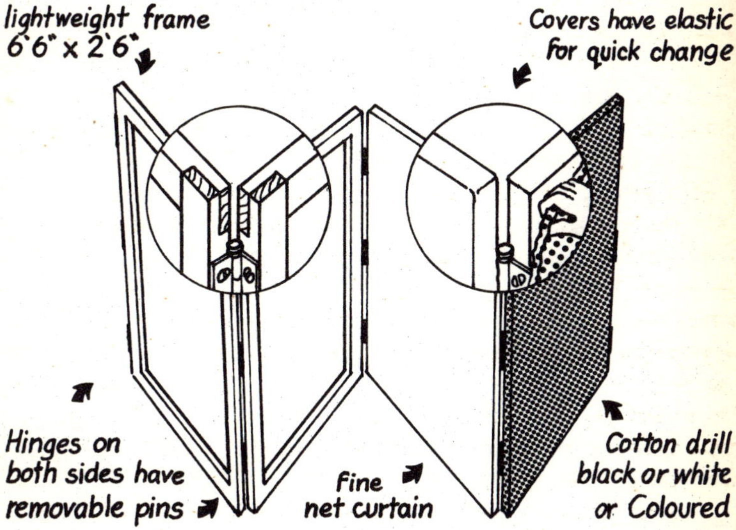

Choose one of the four ideas in the picture below and write down the bare outline of a story around it. You have fifteen minutes.

....

Screen Usage

(*The screens may also be used to display posters advertising church events.*)

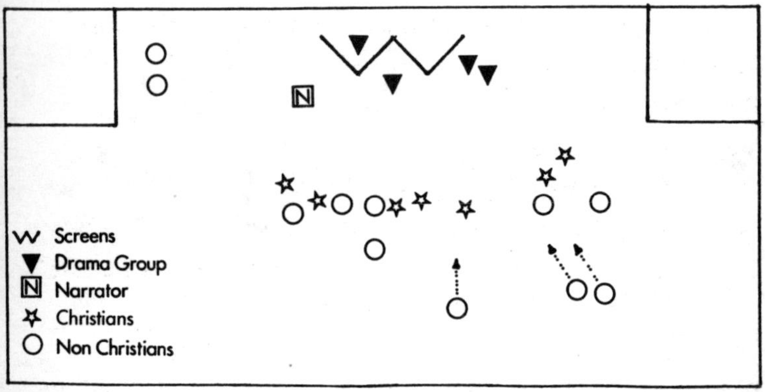

3. Performance

The spot where you choose to perform can make a big difference. Try to find somewhere which provides a natural backdrop: a wall, a fence, railings or a hedge. (Try to avoid standing under trees - unless you are prepared to risk falling bird droppings!) There should be enough room for you and the public without blocking pavements or shop doorways. The sun should be in your eyes, not in the audience's. Do not wear sunglasses unless you are playing a character who needs them.

When acting in the open air you must remember to:

* project your voice

* build a rapport with the onlookers

* make sure entrances and exits are well polished

* ignore any hecklers

* attract a crowd for the preacher

After the open air the drama group should get together to review, as realistically as possible, how things went. This can be done at the first rehearsal of the next drama.

THE BOX SKETCH

Cast: 2 people - one of whom has a cardboard box on his head.

Man Hello!

Box Hi!

Man How are you doin'?

Box Oh fine. Beautiful day, isn't it?

Man Yeah, I love it when the sun shines.

Box You're not serious! You don't really believe all that stuff about the sun shining, do you?

Man Of course I do. And today it's really shining.

Box I didn't think anyone believed in that stuff about the sun shining any more.

Man Well, I didn't always believe. There was a time when I thought it was a load of rubbish.

Box What made you change your mind?

Man Well, you see, I had this box on my head - but I didn't know it. I thought I could see everything but I couldn't. In fact, I couldn't see a thing! It was just dark!

Box What happened then?

Man Someone came up to me and told me that I could see the sun shining if I took the box off my head.

Box Oh yeah. So you're trying to tell me I've got a box on my head. You people are crazy. You're the one with the box on your head!

Man Hold on! Hold on! You can know for yourself. Right now if you just change your mind and let me take the box off your head, you'll be able to see everything. Just change your thinking.

Box Go on then - but it won't work.

(Man lifts box off other's head)

Box Oh wow! I can see everything! Look, the sun's shining. This is incredible!

(Exit Man)

(Another person comes along with a box on his head. The ex-box man approaches him.)

Ex-Box Hey! Hey! The sun actually is shining but you've just got a box on your head.

Box Look, get lost. You people make me sick. You're a weirdo, a fanatic. Leave me alone.

(Exit Box)

Chapter Six
PREACHING

He (Jesus) said to them, "Go into all the world and preach the good news to all creation ..." (Mark 16:15).

' ... the disciples went out and preached everywhere ... ' (Mark 16:20).

The Scriptures call God's people:

witnesses	Acts 1:8
....	2 Cor 5:20
....	2 Cor 6:1

GOD IS LOOKING FOR MESSENGERS

As heralds of the King, we are all commissioned to deliver a message. If we are not prepared to speak, how can anyone believe the gospel and be saved (Romans 10:13-15)? The poor are waiting to hear it. The prisoners are longing to be set free. The blind crave their sight and the oppressed are crying out for release. They are all on our doorstep, all without Christ and all on their way to hell.

It is clear from the Scriptures, however, that although every Christian is a witness, not all are expected to be evangelists. Evangelists, like apostles, prophets, pastors and teachers, are specially appointed by God (Ephesians 4:11). So although everyone should at least be *willing* to preach Jesus in an open air setting, not everyone should do so.

> The greatest men should always be the evangelists, and generally have been; and the idea that Tom, Dick and Harry can be put up to speak on a street corner, but you must have a great preacher in a pulpit in a

church is, to me, the reversing of the right order.

(Martyn Lloyd- Jones)

How do you feel about allowing any Christian to preach the gospel in the open air?

....

....

....

....

....

To what extent should women be involved in open air preaching is an obvious question. From a purely practical angle, we tend to feel that men are probably better able to cope with the direct attacks of hecklers than women. In addition, men usually have the strongest voices and are more likely to be heard above the general street clamour. The theological argument about whether women should preach on the street, we leave for you to decide. There is certainly no reason why a lady should not give a personal testimony in the open air. How do you feel about allowing women to preach the gospel in the open air?

....

....

....

....

....

Now let us suppose that you have been asked to speak at the next open air meeting. Either you can forget about it until the event descends on you and then panic! Or you can prepare from an early date and allow God to shape the message with you. If you are consistently open to the Father's leading and work hard, the results will have to be good. C. H. Spurgeon put it another way: 'Pray as though it all depends on God. Preach as though it all depends on you.'

MESSENGERS WITH A BIBLICAL MESSAGE

In an open air you have up to seven minutes to preach the gospel. Clearly this is not sufficient time to go into great detail so you will need to know what to include and what to leave out. To stuff your talk full of superb illustrations is only good news if you have time to give them a spiritual application. If you don't, you may succeed in touching people's emotions but not their wills.

Evangelistic preaching should be characterised by four main themes: Sin, Jesus, Faith and Repentance. We need to have a clear understanding of each before we speak so let's look at them.

1. Sin.

a) What is sin? .... (1 John 5:17)

b) How did sin enter the world?

.... (Rom 5:12)

c) How did people become sinners?

.... (Rom 5:19)

d) How many good people are there alive today?

.... (Rom 3:10-12)

(It is important to understand that we have sinful 'roots' before we concentrate on the more apparent 'weeds' that grow out of them.)

e) What obvious sins emerge from the secret sinful nature?

....

....

.... (Gal 5:19-21)

f) What is the result of sin? .... (Rom 6:23)

2. Jesus

a) Divinity

(i) Write out John 1:1

....

....

(ii) What dwells in Jesus?

.... (Col 1:19)

Jesus confirmed His divinity through His sinlessness, His miracles and His resurrection.

b) Death

What has God done for us through the physical death of Jesus?

....

....

.... (Col 1:21-22)

c) Resurrection

Where would we be if Jesus had not been raised from the dead?

.... (1 Cor 15:17)

3. Faith

a) Correct the following statement:

' ... it is by grace you have been saved, through faith - and this is from yourselves ... '

....

....

.... (Eph 2:8)

b) What must you believe to be saved?

(i) . ... that I am a sinner

(ii) .... that God loves me

(iii) .... that Jesus died to take away my sins

(iv) .... that I must repent and seek forgiveness from Him

What Bible references would you use to support each of these statements?

(i) ....

(ii) ....

(iii) ....

(iv) ....

4. Repentance

When someone repents he 'changes his mind or his thinking'. Instead of believing that he is basically 'not a bad chap really', he adopts God's view of himself. He realises that he is a sinner and turns away from his sin. Unless he has been brought to the point of acknowledging and confessing his sinfulness, he cannot be saved.

What will happen to a sinner if he refuses to repent?

.... (Luke 13:5)

MESSENGERS WITH A PREPARED MESSAGE

A good message grows. It usually begins with a thought (a verse of Scripture) and develops further structure as you think around it. Give yourself time to find out what God wants to say and pray about it. Carry a notebook around so that when you get an idea you can immediately write it down. (If you jot down illustrations or quotations whenever you hear them, you will find them an invaluable reference source in the future).

Read 2 Timothy 4:2
What is Timothy told to preach? ....

If you preach on a theme, you may get carried away in it. By all means refer to things like abortion, money and the struggle for power but never allow any of these to become central. 'What God says' is what the world needs to hear so base your message on a particular verse or passage of Scripture (e.g. John 14:6, Matthew 7:13,14). It should be simple, jargon-free and relevant to the people you are talking to. It will require a definite beginning, middle and end and the points you make should contain structure and build on one another. If you have a clear prepared outline in mind when you speak, you will remember what you want to say next. And those listening will appreciate a well- organised message more than a general ramble with a couple of Scripture verses tacked on at the end!

When you know what you want to say, it is a good idea to practise it on someone who has a degree of experience in public speaking. If you know that another Christian has approved of your approach, your confidence will increase. You will also be able to see, through his eyes, how your message might be misinterpreted. Once you have satisfied yourself that you have the finished product, practise it repeatedly and commit the whole thing to memory. You will not be using any notes in the open air.

If you would like to consider using a visual aid in your presentation, a sketchboard will provide an excellent continuous visual reference point. For more information on how to use one, have a look at Graham Simms' very practical book, *Preaching and Painting the Gospel*. It is available from Open Air Campaigners.

MESSENGERS WITH A CLEAR MESSAGE

The Holy Spirit can use the poorest preacher and win souls through him. This fact, however, should not encourage you to be casual about how you present the material. When you speak, people will not just be listening to a verbal message, they will be encountering a person.

You will communicate before you speak. Your appearance and manner will do that for you. Super-smart or sensationally scruffy clothing is probably not a good idea! And if you come across with a superior attitude, few will stay long to hear you out.

Try to be relaxed and natural when you move and speak. Always have a good opening sentence - attention quickly gained is easily retained. If you begin where people are, you will have an advantage so catch and hold interest by referring to a world event, a public tragedy, or a current topic of conversation. Work quickly from that into a gospel message.

Read the following verses and find a good opening line to introduce a gospel message for each one.

Example: Luke 19:10 - Have you ever been lost?

Matt 11:4,5 ....

Rom 1:16 ....

Rom 3:23 ....

2 Cor 5:21 ....

If you look at people when you speak to them, you are more likely to build up a rapport with them. Project your voice. You are competing with transport, marching feet, shop music, ghetto blasters, general bustle and conversation. Avoid repeating yourself; pause periodically and vary your voice so that it does not become monotonous. Be compassionate but be confident and positive too. Above all, be enthusiastic. If you believe what you are saying it should show.

When you come to the end of your message, finish! What do you want interested people to do? (Take a leaflet from Sue? Talk to one of the team afterwards? Come forward for prayer for healing?) Make sure that you tell the group in advance what is going to happen or you may find yourself alone to deal with all the follow-up.

Find a large piece of paper and work out an open air message based on John 14:6 - 'I am the way and the truth and the life'. Make sure that it has a good introduction, three clear points and a definite finish.

Chapter Seven
LITERATURE

The world could teach us a lot about marketing. A good company sales manager knows that his product will sell only if it is presented to the general public in an effective form. That's why he consults with his advisers who, in turn, arrange for consumer research to be carried out. When the advertisements, handbills and vouchers are printed, they reflect the careful thought that has been put into them. The marketing team considers exactly where any leaflets should be distributed and sees that they end up in the hands of those who are likely to respond. When sales figures rise, the management knows that its advertising campaign has been successful.

Christians are presenting a Person to the world. When they hand out leaflets they are saying, 'Please read this. We want you to know Jesus.' Jesus is honoured when His people take time to consider what sort of literature will interest today's society and then produce it for them.

Although there are several good ready-printed leaflets that you can buy, you will often do better to create your own. This is because no one can know your 'market' better than you. You live among the people, you are aware of their age ranges/educational ability/wealth and you understand the greatest needs of your area.

What sort of people live in your neighbourhood?

....

....

....

....

EFFECTIVE COMMUNICATION

If you work hard at something, the chances are that it will turn out well. Effective literature only communicates effectively when you put a lot of thought behind it. You need to know what sort of leaflets you want, what goes into them and when to approach the general public.

There are five basic kinds of leaflet/tract:

Advertisement

Story

Testimony

Questionnaire

Gospel

They have been listed here in ascending order of the amount of conversation about Jesus that each will probably involve.

1. Advertisement

When you hand someone an invitation to a Christian event you probably will not share much of the gospel message with him. At this stage your goal will be to be friendly and to encourage him to come along to the event. Hopefully if he does turn up you will get the chance to talk to him before he goes home or (depending on what time the event finishes) on some future occasion.
Write down some ideas for an evangelistic church function

e.g. barbecue ....

....

....

The invitation (like any tract) should suit the person it is for. Children love bright colours, but these are not so essential for adults. Elderly people often find it hard to read small print and in certain areas, some people find it hard to read at all. Illustrations or borders usually improve appearance, as do colour changes. This healing guest service invitation card was green and blue.

You are invited to a

HEALING GUEST SERVICE

at Clarendon Church
Clarendon Villas, Hove
on Sunday 27th March
at 7.30pm

The evening will consist of a time of worship, drama, a short talk and prayer for the sick

Make sure that the following details are included on any invitation:

* date
* time
* location
* what is happening

The following information may also be useful:

* map (particularly if the city/town is large)
* contact phone number (possibly church office)

2. Story

Well-written and illustrated story-type tracts are very effective. They capture the imagination by approaching the gospel from an interesting angle. Instead of beginning with the Bible, they use a story/cartoon/analogy to illustrate a point and then bring in a Salvation message. Jesus' parables and references to topical events are good examples of this method.

Look up the following, say what each example is about and state the truth it contains:

Luke 10:30-37

Parable: ....

Truth: ....

Luke 13:1-5

Event: ....

Truth: ....

What human problems could you describe in story/analogy/cartoon form? (eg loneliness, rebellion, lostness)

....

....

....

Now write down some current major news items/topical themes (e.g. AIDS, catastrophes, Easter, Christmas)

....

....

....

When producing this sort of tract, use a catchy title which relates to the opening theme (eg 'In the dark?', 'Help!', 'Fearful?', 'Two Birthdays', 'Alive from the Dead'). If you want to relate the tract to a current topic, be very careful that you do not make a complex issue sound simple and then draw an analogy from it. Also refrain from commenting negatively about other religions or types of people. Make sure too that you do not over-order any current event tracts. If you do decide to produce 5,000 for the general election, you do not want to have 3,654 left over after everyone has voted!

3. Testimony

a) From the Church

A local church leaflet does two things: it shares how people's lives have been changed and invites the reader to the church to learn more about the God who changed them. The literature can be handed out in the town with or without much one to one conversation.

Central Brighton has many attractions: department stores and supermarkets; places of entertainment; culinary delights; beautiful public gardens; a wealth of historical landmarks; in a word, character.

There are also, to be fair, some things we'd rather not be reminded of: vast crowds of shoppers; high prices; and double yellow lines, to name just a few.

Life can be discouraging, too, Friends can let us down, our hopes can be dashed, and our plans defeated.

Inside, you can read about two lives that were being spoiled, in very different ways, and how a meeting with the Living God has put the pieces back together again.

You will need to include the following in this sort of leaflet:

* An interesting introduction
* Two or three different testimonies
* Photos of the 'testimony' Christians
* A map to show people how to get to the church
* The times of the Sunday meetings/services
* A phone for enquiries

Using the front page of the 'Brighton' leaflet as an example, write down some ideas for an introduction to a leaflet which you could use in your area.

....

....

....

....

....

....

Before you ask anyone to produce a church leaflet testimony, think. Are you really looking for three conversion accounts? Why not have two and make the third a story about someone in your fellowship who was healed (preferably after one of your meetings)? The conversion testimonies will need to be thorough but not too 'revealing'. If you focus on specific sins, they can easily take centre stage and this is something you want to avoid.

It is an excellent idea to have a mixture of people, in terms of age, sex, occupation (or further education, maybe even long-term unemployment) and possibly nationality (especially if you live in a multi-racial area). Make the testimonies relevant to the reader. On many housing estates it would probably be inappropriate to feature a university student, a bank manager and an olympic skier! Similarly, in a stockbroker belt, your public would probably not be able to relate well to a dustman, a farmer's wife and an ex-convict. In certain areas there may be two very well-defined age groupings and you could find yourself preparing two tracts to accommodate, say, the elderly and the young. You may decide to do this anyway.

The conversion testimonies will be more interesting if they come from different angles. One could lean more on 'becoming a Christian' while the other could work from when a person believed but major on what God has done since conversion. Incidentally, the testimonies do not need to be written by the Christians concerned. They may find it hard to be fluent on paper and yet, at the end of the day, refuse to allow anyone to improve their efforts! To avoid this, it might be better for someone to conduct interviews and write the testimonies down for them. Alternatively, if the individual does want to compose his own story, make sure that he is willing for it to be altered if necessary. Each testimony needs to be about two hundred well-edited words in length.

b) From You

Personal tracts are powerful weapons. A person cannot easily dismiss your written testimony when he has spoken to you in real life. Even if you have not had the opportunity to share the gospel with him, your friendliness will have been apparent. When you hand him a personal tract, you are explaining that God's love is the motivation behind your friendly attitude. You need a well-thought out tract to do it.

Before you begin to write your testimony down, pray for wisdom and clarity, then read Acts 26:4-23. It is evident from these verses that the apostle Paul built his testimony round three main points:

* Before he became a Christian
* How he became a Christian
* After he became a Christian

It's an excellent structure. You tell people how you used to live, how God met you and how your life changed as a result.

Write brief notes on what you were like before you became a Christian and how you changed afterwards

Before ....

....

....

How ....

....

....

After ....

....

....

Talk through your story with a friend who makes fairly detailed notes on what you say. You should be able to produce a rough draft from these notes and any additional thoughts. If it doesn't sound right, change it until it does. Your time will not be wasted.

Now read the rough copy and listen out for something in it which you want to emphasise and which will make your tract more interesting to read. If you have been healed, maybe you would like to draw attention to that. If God has delivered you from fear, loneliness

or financial problems you could run that particular theme through your story. Don't try to be clever. People will relate only to people who are 'real'.
Can you think of any theme that could run through your testimony?

....

Next take your rough draft and fit it around your chosen theme. You will need to remove any unnecessary details, add new ones and ensure that Jesus is central to what you want to say. Start with a good first sentence (eg 'I made a real mess of my life') and include a Scripture verse because the Word of God is powerful in its own right. Your final draft should be no more than three hundred words long.

As you write, remember to:

* be yourself:	write in a chatty style - as a friend might
* be simple:	avoid jargon (eg redemption, repentance, atoning sacrifice, blessed, gloriously saved etc) and difficult vocabulary
* be genuine:	don't over-emphasise how bad you used to be
* be accurate:	truth convicts so there is no need to exaggerate
* be realistic:	you don't stop having problems but God helps you through them
* be careful:	try not to confuse the reader by using 'God' one minute and 'Jesus' the next
* be positive:	don't knock other Christians or churches

When you have finished working on the final copy, show it to someone who will make some useful comments. Don't be surprised if you need to alter it here and there. An outsider will probably see things that you have not noticed so welcome his suggestions.

Your personal tract should be printed on coloured card (size A6). The catchy title at the top of the first page should reflect the theme of your testimony (eg 'I Found It!', 'Healed!', 'No Longer Alone', 'A Fresh Start'). Your photo will go under the heading and your testimony should begin on the same page so that the non-Christian will be encouraged to turn over and read on. A contact address or phone number at the end of the tract may be useful but do not use your church office number unless you have permission to do so. It is perhaps wiser if women do not give an address or phone number. They can write these in a space at the end of the tract if appropriate to a particular situation.

purpose which has not left me. I felt accepted by God and many emotional hurts have been healed by His mighty, loving power.

More recently, He has healed me of a troublesome asthmatic condition. Nothing is too difficult for God. He can heal and change you, too!

Claire Turner

page 4

SET FREE FROM

ANOREXIA!

Trapped!

That was me....as a teenager, I could not live up to the image of myself. So I thought 'why bother?' I felt depressed and a failure, so I stopped eating. I became very thin and

page 1

List the names of ten people you know to whom you could give a personal tract.

1. .... 6. ....
2. .... 7. ....
3. .... 8. ....
4. .... 9. ....
5. .... 10. ....

suffered from *anorexia nervosa*, the so-called 'slimmer's disease'.

My friends, my family and even the psychiatrist failed to help me; the more they tried to build up my self-confidence, the further I retreated into my shell.

New Relationship

I met up again with an old school friend, who had since become a Christian. She had a security and purpose to life, and I realised that these were the very things I lacked. Her genuine relationship with Jesus Christ intrigued me. She introduced me to other Christians from her church, and they seemed to care about one another.

page 2

They didn't try to change me, but accepted me for who I was. Eventually, I cried out to God. 'If you're really there, please come and change me!' I wanted to find the peace and security I had seen in the Christians I had met. God visited me there and then, forgiving me for my rebellion and apathy towards Him, replacing my self-centredness with a concern for others, and breathing new life into me.

Ten Years On

From that moment, God radically changed me. I started to eat properly, began to like other people and became more outgoing. I experienced an inner peace and

page 3

Now list ten situations when you could give a personal tract to someone you have spoken to briefly (eg at the petrol station, at the bus stop)

1. ....

2. ....

3. ....

4. ....

5. ....

6. ....

7. ....

8. ....

9. ....

10. ....

4. Questionnaire

A survey is not the same thing as a questionnaire. If you conduct a survey, you are gathering data with the intention of producing an end result (eg 80% of those interviewed believed in God). If you want to find out people's opinions you will carry out a questionnaire and you need do nothing with the information you collect. When you talk to individuals on the street, you are usually not really interested in producing survey information. Your questionnaire acts more as a tool which you hope will lead into a conversation about Jesus.

Once you have written your questionnaire and had it printed, secure it to a clipboard and carry it out in pairs. Two men should approach a man, and two women another woman. The more experienced/confident of the pair should ask the questions while the other prays silently and learns. When the roles are reversed the trainee individual will have someone to back him/her up if the going gets tough. At a later stage you may prefer to work individually with the questionnaires.

There is a greater skill behind the asking of the questions than meets the eye. You will need to be sensitive to the individual as you speak to him. When he says he believes in God, accept his answer and press on. Your goal is to lead to the question, 'If you could know God, would you be interested?' If he would, you can show him how he can find a relationship with God by sharing with him a tract which outlines the way of salvation (eg *Knowing God Personally*). If he is not interested, suggest casually that one day he might feel a greater desire for God and hand him the tract anyway. As he leaves pray that he will think again about your conversation with him, reconsider his answers and even (out of curiosity) read the literature.

Role Play

Get together with a Christian friend and practise the New Frontiers' Questionnaire on one another.

Now find a non-Christian friend and ask him/her to answer the questions.

New Frontiers Questionnaire

Interviewer ....

Date .... (ring answers as appropriate)

Fe/Male

Do you have any religious background? ....

Do you belong to a church? Yes/No

How often do you attend? Frequently Seldom Never

Do you think the Bible's teaching is out of date? Yes/No

How often do you read it? Frequently Seldom Never

Is there more to you than just body and mind? If so, what?

Which best describes you?

1. Definitely believe in God
2. Think I do - but not sure
3. Sometimes
4. Not at all

What do you believe will happen to you when you die?

1. Reincarnation
2. Cease to exist
3. Hell
4. Heaven (eternal life)
5. Don't know
6. Other (Specify)

Can a person know he or she is going to heaven?
Yes/ No/ Don't know.

Do you have a satisfying purpose in life? If so, what?

....

What do you want most out of life? ....

What do you think is THE basic problem of man?

1. Greed & materialism
2. Selfishness
3. Violence, fighting, war
4. Pride, sin, hate
5. Don't know
6. Other (specify)

What is sin? ....

Are you a sinner? Yes/ No/ Don't know

How can you get rid of your sin? ....

Who do you say Jesus Christ is?

1. The Son of God
2. A good man, teacher
3. A mythical person
4. Don't know
5. Other (Specify)

Why did He die?

1. Because He broke the law
2. Deliberately for our sins
3. Don't know
4. Other (Specify)

Did He rise again from the dead? Yes/ No/ Don't know

In your opinion, how does a person become a Christian?

1. Believe in Christ as personal Saviour
2. Join a church
3. A person is brought up a Christian
4. Live a good life
5. Believe in God
6. Don't know
7. Other (Specify)

Do you believe God is interested in you personally?
Yes/ No/ Don't know

Does God let everyone into heaven no matter what?
Yes/ No/ Don't know

If you were to die and stand before God and He were to ask you 'Why should I let you into my heaven?' what would you say?

....

If you could know God personally would you be interested?
Yes/ No/ Don't know

Can you ignore God forever? Yes/No

5. Gospel

Gospel tracts often take the form of booklets which run through the steps you need to take to become a Christian. Since there are several good ones on the market already (eg *Journey into Life, Knowing God Personally* and *Bridge to Life*) you will probably not be able to improve on them. Although you might prefer more up-to-date illustrations, it is probably not worth the expense of designing new ones when the essential material remains the same. You can, however, invest valuable time researching what gospel tracts are available and in choosing the approach which best suits the type of people to whom you are likely to talk.

Because gospel booklets emphasise the message of salvation for everyone, they can lose something of a personal touch. The gap is ideally filled when a Christian comes alongside an unbeliever and works through the gospel with him, applying the truth to his particular circumstances. This sort of one to one contact is naturally the most intensive, effective - and, when the listener is keen to learn, the most enjoyable to do. Once the unbeliever has been shown the gospel he can take the booklet home, remind himself from it of what he needs to do and make his decision.

Role Play

For practice, go through a gospel booklet with a friend, taking it in turns to be the 'Christian'.

EFFECTIVE CONTACT

It's one thing to have good literature but another to pass it on effectively. Before you go out, consider and act on the following:

a) Avoid all contact with garlic/onions etc for two hours before the open air!

b) Dress casually but not scruffily

c) Be friendly when you approach people

d) Know what's in the literature you have with you so that you can distribute it wisely

e) Don't give literature to people while they are standing watching the open air

f) Do give literature to people who are walking away from the open air or who are passing and do not intend to stop

g) Talk to people whenever you can (ie don't let literature distribution become an excuse for not opening your mouth)

h) Arrange for a couple of questionnaires to be done about fifty metres from the open air site

i) Carry your personal testimony tract wherever you go

Can you think of any other useful things to remember?

....

....

....

Useful address for literature: CPO Head Office, Garcia Estate, Canterbury Road, Worthing, West Sussex, BN13 1BW.

Chapter Eight
ONE-TO-ONE

Imagine yourself at a Saturday morning open air in your town. You are familiar with the surroundings, aware of the weather and conscious of a multitude of shoppers all milling around everywhere. There's the roar of traffic, an ambulance siren and the cry of the street seller declaring his prices to the world.

Now imagine Jesus in His open air work. There's sand, heat, and bustle everywhere. There are children crying, beggars begging, sellers selling. The humidity and the press of the crowds around Jesus make it almost impossible for Him to breathe, let along eat. Inside every heart there is a pressing need that only Jesus can meet. They call to Him for help: 'My daughter has just died. But come and put your hand on her ...' (Matt 9:18); 'If I only touch his cloak, I will be healed' (Matt 9:21); 'Jesus, Son of David, have mercy on me!' (Mark 10:47)

Why didn't Jesus wave a hand in the general direction of the person needing help and offer a quick but effective prayer? He, of all people, could not afford the time to stop and deal with specific requests, to draw a man away from the crowd to heal him, to lift little children onto His lap. But He did all of these things. Why? Because He was concerned for individuals.

Give two examples from the Gospels of Jesus' concern for individuals (eg Luke 8:26-33).

....

....

When you look out over the Saturday morning crowd, remember that the people you see are individuals. Hidden by the self-confident expression, the way-out hairstyle, the purposeful walk, the old raincoat, is a human being who is unconsciously crying out to Jesus for help: 'My son is ill; my back is killing me; does anyone care?'

If we view an open air as an opportunity to reach out to crowds alone, we are missing the point. Just as Jesus had time for one-to-one contact, so have we. The goal is not to pace through the event as quickly as possible, get out of the cold and go home. It's to meet the needs of individuals without Christ - and that costs a little more.

If the individual contact with people is so important, how should it be done? What's the best way to approach a complete stranger? How do you start a conversation? What should you say? How do you finish? The questions whirl round and threaten a big panic - both for those handing out the leaflets and for the others when the open air meeting is over. Wouldn't it help if you had some idea of the answers to these questions before you went out on the street?

1. PATTERN IN THE PAST

For a working example of how one man approached and began talking to a complete stranger, read Acts 8:26-40.

Now answer the following questions:

a) Why was Philip walking alone along a desert road?

....

....

b) Why did he approach the eunuch's chariot?

....

....

c) Who began the conversation?

....

d) Who told him to begin the conversaton?

....

e) What was the opening line?

....

....

f) Was there a positive or a negative reaction to it?

....

g) Where did Philip begin his explanation of the gospel?

....

....

h) What did he preach?

....

i) Did the eunuch understand? How do we know?

....

....

Now look up Psalm 68:31. It is widely believed that the eunuch fulfilled this prophecy by being the first evangelist to Ethiopia. If this is true, Philip evidently played a crucial part in leading him to Christ. You could be used in a similar way.

2. PRACTICE IN THE PRESENT

a) Prompting and Approach

Philip obeyed the voice of the angel and the prompting of the Spirit. He was therefore in the right place at the right time. Since the chariot would almost certainly have been well-guarded, his decision to approach a eunuch probably took a lot of courage.

The prompting of the Spirit still comes to Christians today. Often you have a 'gut feeling' that you should talk to a particular onlooker. On other occasions, God will arrange events so that you end up chatting to the right person almost without realising it. Even if you do not receive a specific 'prod' to speak to anyone, go ahead anyway. If Philip had waited for God to tell him to question the eunuch, he might have been running alongside the chariot for hours! Having been brought thus far, it was a matter of common sense that he should start up a conversation. You don't need to wait for a spiritual experience from on high before you open your mouth! You are a witness, so you must be willing to speak.

Let's suppose that you are free to talk to someone. If you're honest, what sort of approach do you think you would be inclined to adopt? Tick your answer.

(i) Skirt round the person and slink up from behind

(ii) Saunter in the general direction of the person not knowing what to say

(iii) Gain eye contact and approach

(iv) March confidently straight up to the person

(v) Lose your nerve and talk to another church member

b) Time to Speak

'Mumble, mumble er ... (gasp), hello ... waffle ... goodbye!' Let's face it, it's not easy to strike up a conversation with a complete stranger. Most people would rather move away or get extremely occupied with packing up the musical instruments. But if everyone finds a reason to avoid talking to the bystanders, who is left to invite them to the Sunday night guest service? Who is left to listen to the sad story of the woman whom God has touched and who is now close to tears? Who is left to give a leaflet to the man who will read it at home and immediately ask Jesus into his life? You?

(i) Be a Good Questioner

You are the human link between God and the world. That's why Jesus has asked you to be His witness. You will need to make a conscious decision that you will not leave the one-to-one work to everyone else. At the end of the open air, take a deep breath, send an arrow prayer to your heavenly Father and plunge in! Philip began by asking the Ethiopian a relevant question. Why not try one of these?

(a) 'Hello! What did you think about what we've been doing?'

(b) 'Hi! May I give you one of these?' (ie. a brightly-coloured leaflet introducing your church)

(c) 'Do you understand what this is all about?'

(d) 'Would you like a balloon?'

(e) 'Who do you think Jesus is?'

Write down others.

....

....

....

....

(ii) Be a Good Listener

How you continue the conversation will depend very much on the sort of response you get. When Paul encountered people who were not interested in his message he turned his attention to those who were (Acts 18:6-8). Don't detain those who don't want to talk but don't expect everyone to be uninterested! The Ethiopian was happy for

Philip to sit beside him and explain the Scriptures. If you encounter the reply, 'What's it all about, then?' or 'You all look very happy,' make the most of the opportunity.

Since people are individuals, conversations will naturally flow from different starting points. The key to making a good contact is to discover where a person is before you launch into what you want to tell him. Philip noticed that the Ethiopian was reading from Isaiah and began from there. So listen to what a person is saying (verbally and non-verbally) and move from that point.

(iii) Be a Good Speaker

Since you probably have only a short time to talk to people, do your best to bring Jesus into the conversation. You may be able to share how you became a Christian (see Ben Davies' book *Effective Evangelism* in this series). Answer genuine questions fairly and avoid jargon unless you explain it. If you want to talk about being 'born again' don't rattle on assuming that your listener looks educated and is therefore bound to understand! Define what you mean in simple language. The high ranking Ethiopian official became a Christian as a result of hearing a very clear message from Philip.

While you are talking, be expectant. Philip was able to lead the Ethiopian to Christ. You may not achieve this goal, but you can make an impact on someone by the way you approach him. If you respect him, you will not insult him or force him to pray a prayer for salvation when he is not ready for the commitment.

Read Matthew 19:21-22. Where did this man's security lie?

....

What did Jesus tell him to do?

....

....

Did Jesus try to stop him? YES/NO

(iv) Be a Good Detective

Some conversations should be finished in the middle! When the discussion begins to go round in circles bring it to a close, thank the individual for his time and move away. If, on the other hand, a conversation has gone well, give the individual some literature (a gospel or a church leaflet), offer to pray for him and/or arrange a further meeting. When you have finished talking, smile and say, 'goodbye'. It means a lot to people. Always leave a person so that another Christian on another occasion will be able to follow on from where you have left off.

Role Play

Try some role play to help you to overcome any fear of one-to-one work that you have. Get together with a friend. One of you is the Christian, the other has been watching some of your open air. The Christian should engage the other in conversation and determine the level of interest in spiritual things. Don't make it too difficult for your partner, because after five minutes you will swap roles.

c) Share the Good News

Be prepared! Some of the people you talk to will be interested in hearing the main points of the gospel message. If you don't want to be stuck for an answer, try this simple, visual method of explaining about God and what Jesus has done for us.

(i) Holy God, Sinful Man

Draw a big letter C with an ellipse at the top and bottom. In the top ellipse write the word 'GOD' and talk about some of his characteristics (creator, holy, true, eternal, loving etc.) Now write the word 'MAN' in the bottom ellipse. Explain that God created man in His own image and that he was able to relate to Him.

Next draw some clouds between the ellipses and mention how sin came into the world and how it creates a barrier between God and man.

GOD
CREATION & RELATIONSHIP
MAN

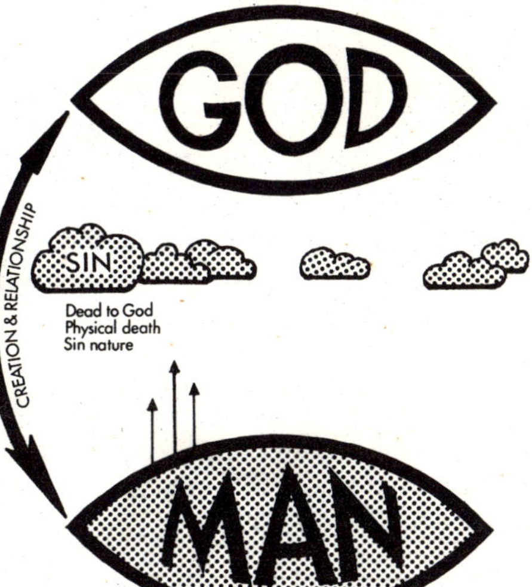
GOD
CREATION & RELATIONSHIP
SIN
Dead to God
Physical death
Sin nature
MAN

Share Romans 3: 23
Write out the verse here.

....

....

Now write down for your listener some of the results of sin. You will find them in the following verses:

Verse	**Result**
Rom 6:23	....
Gal 5:19-21	....
	....
	....
	....
	....

You will not need to write down all of the results of sin for your listener! While you are talking, have an ear open to God and try sensitively to work out what sort of sins are most appropriate to mention to him. Remember, though, that these sins are the consequence of a sinful nature and that the person needs forgiveness for being a sinner and not just for doing bad things. Make it clear therefore that everyone is totally sinful and corrupt before God. You might even shade the bottom ellipse to contrast man's wickednesswith God's purity.

(ii) Man Cannot Reach God

Now draw in the arrows which reach up from man towards God (see previous diagram). Explain that man tries to find purpose and fulfilment in life in many different ways: materialism, relationships, a 'worthy cause' (eg rights for the poor, save the whale), politics, even religion (good deeds and churchgoing!) Again try to find the most apt illustrations for your hearer. If he's obviously a music fanatic, state 'music', and if he looks like a businessman, state 'career'.

Tell your listener that no matter how hard he tries, he cannot find total fulfilment in anything until he finds God. And he cannot reach God until his sin has been dealt with. If he tries to lean on his good works, share with him Ephesians 2:8,9 and the first few words of Galatians 2:16. Once you have made clear the hopelessness of your hearer's situation, begin to share the good news of Jesus

(iii) God Reaches Man

Tell your hearer that although he cannot reach God, God has provided a way to reach him. Share from John 3:16 how the Father loves people and sent His Son to save them. Draw a large arrow running down the centre of the diagram. Explain that Jesus led a sinless life and that when He was crucified He took on Himself the sin of the world.

Now draw the cross which acts as the only bridge between God and need.

Write out what Jesus said here:

....

.... (John 14:6)

Go on to describe what Jesus did at the cross and how He satisfied the Father's anger against sin. Make it clear to your listener that he can be forgiven if he repents and believes that Jesus died for him (1 John 1:9). Explain that if he does this he will not only receive a new nature, but eternal life as well. Complete the circle by drawing in the arrow on the right.

Ensure that he understands that commitment to Christ will cost him everything and ask him if he would like to become a Christian. If so, lead him in a simple prayer for salvation which should run something like this:

Lord Jesus, thank You for loving me.
I admit that I am a sinner and am truly sorry for all the things I have done wrong.
I believe that You died on the cross for me.
I want to give my life back to You.
Please come into my life right now, forgive me and change me.
Thank You, Jesus.
Amen

Turn to Romans 10:9,10 and encourage him to believe that Jesus has heard his prayer and that he is saved. Take his full name and address and make sure that there is definite follow up within the next seven days.

If the individual does not want to make a commitment now, leave him with some literature, ask for his name and address and invite him to come along to church.

Role Play

Find a Christian friend and practise sharing this gospel outline with him. Take it in turns to play the 'Christian' and then the 'interested unbeliever'.

Pray for opportunities to share this outline with at least one person this week.

Chapter Nine
PRAISE MARCHES

Excitement is nearly always generated when a large number of individuals come together to do something. As the Olympic teams file past at the start of the Games, you can feel the electric atmosphere and see the enthusiasm written on faces everywhere. Even on home territory, if you become aware that there is some sort of gathering at the end of your street, you immediately want to know more. Your curiosity either has you outside and walking up the road or peering through an upstairs window.

A crowd draws a crowd. If you want to make a major impact on your area, go for a large scale open air. It will involve a lot of organisation but you will find it tremendously enjoyable and very worthwhile.

The next two chapters cover four larger open air events. They are:

* Praise March
* Fun Day
* Town Arts Festival
* Procession

There are probably others too. You may wish to plan something around an annual village celebration. In this case you might consider some of the ideas here and adapt them to suit that function.

PRAISE MARCH

When the church of the past has taken to the streets, the procession has tended to be conducted in silence. The event has been known by church members as 'a march of witness' or a 'march which demonstrates for human rights'. Sometimes it co-incides with a

Christian festival, usually it is a relatively solemn occasion - particularly if the participants are following a large cross. The emphasis is on meditation and the public sees how 'sincere' the church is in its mission.

If the man in the street always sees Christianity as something supremely serious, he will never see its relevance for him. If, on the other hand, he is confronted with a large procession of cheerful colourful individuals all singing, shouting and proclaiming the truths of God along his high street, his reaction is likely to be totally different. When we go out on a praise march, we are telling the world that God is worth knowing and that His people are the happiest on earth. Praise marches are not alien to Scripture.

Look up 1 Chronicles 15:25-29

Who was in the procession?

.... (v 28a)

How did they express their joy?

....

....

....

.... (v 28b)

What were David, the Levites and the singers wearing?

.... (v 27)

A similar jubilation was evident when Jesus entered Jerusalem. But shouldn't this march have been the most solemn in all history? Jesus knew that He would soon be going to His death so shouldn't He have taken the Pharisees' advice and calmed the crowds? Shouldn't He have asked them to be respectfully grave and pensive? Not at all! He gladly received the joy of the people. They shouted, waved palm branches in the air, spread their cloaks in front of Him and joyfully praised God in 'loud voices' for all the miracles they had seen. The city was in complete uproar and even the stones threatened to cry out!

If we become this excited about our praise marches, our whole neighbourhood will be stirred to ask the same question as the Israelites in Jerusalem, 'Who is this?' (that you are so enthusiastic about). The same answer applies now as it did then - 'This is Jesus' (Matt 21:11).

1. Participants

The 'entire house of Israel' was involved in King David's procession (2 Sam 6:15) and the whole of Jerusalem was stirred when Jesus entered it (Matt 21:10). Praise marches are not just for the 'keen few' but for everyone. Give your children something to look forward to! Encourage the older members of your church to come along - if only for a hundred yards! The bigger the procession, the greater the impact, the louder the praise, the more exalted our God!

Naturally there will have to be someone who is in overall charge of everything.The chief musician could arrange everything himself for a fairly small march. However, if numbers are in the hundreds it would probably be kinder to lay full responsibility on the shoulders of someone else. The chief musician will have enough on his plate organising the music, songs and rehearsals.

A praise march will involve the following participants:

* Musicians
* Singers
* Outriders
* Rubbish Collectors

a) Musicians

Read again 1 Chronicles 15:27,28. There are four kinds of 'instruments' which the Israelites used to praise God. Write each down in the right category:

Category	**'Instruments'**
Brass	....
Voice	....
Strings	....
Percussion	....

Now translate these instruments into modern day equivalents (if necessary). Be practical - make sure your suggestions are portable!

Category	**'Instruments'**
Brass	....
Voice	....
Strings	....
Percussion	....

The music will be co-ordinated by the main musician and a snare drum. In smaller praise marches you should space the guitarists along one side of the singers so that the sound of their instruments is not muffled. In larger ones you will need to link the lead guitarist's voice and instrument to a mobile P.A. system (which can be hired). The P.A. car should preferably be a hatchback/estate. The amplifier inside it can be driven by a spare car battery or be connected to the cigarette lighter. The P.A. horns (which point forward and back) can be mounted on a roofrack or over a sun roof. The main musician can wear a headpiece microphone and walk behind the car.

b) Singers

Graham Kendrick has written some excellent praise march material. The music leader should choose about six of these songs and get everyone to repeat them, and the rhythmic shouting, until the march ends.

There should be at least three song rehearsals. The best time to practise is on Sunday mornings during the worship time when most people will be around. The music leaders should teach the songs and run through the entire programme with the church. The week before the praise march, the church members should be given the words of the songs/shouts in the order in which they will be sung/shouted. The route should then be made clear to them.

c) Outriders

The outriders walk on either side of the procession. They give out literature to the shoppers/residents and balloons to their children.

Several of them could be dressed up as clowns - it adds to the carnival atmosphere.

d) Rubbish Collectors

In large praise marches there is likely to be a problem with rubbish, Christians do not normally throw litter in the street (do they?!) but children often drop things and tissues do occasionally fall out of sleeves. In addition, tracts are sometimes screwed up by onlookers. The rubbish collectors should be issued with large black plastic bin liners and walk along behind everyone else. They should 'see to' anything that looks remotely 'dropped' and may even do the council road sweepers an added service by going beyond the call of duty ...! What would you like to do at a praise march?

....

(i) RESIDENTIAL PRAISE MARCH

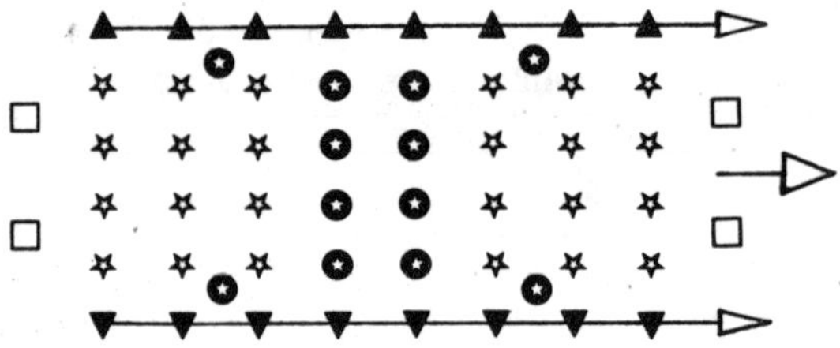

● Musicians

✡ Singers

□ Banners

▼ Outriders (to give sweets and balloons to children and put literature through doors and hand it to passers by)

To be effective it needs 100-200 people (4 or 5 abreast)

2. Programme

a) How to go

Before you become involved in the preparation of a praise march, pray and ask God to help you make the best decisions. It's far better to bring God into your planning from the word 'go' than to slot Him in once you've made up your mind what you want to do.

(ii) CENTRAL TOWN PRAISE MARCH

P.A. Estate car (1 main guitarist with both voice and guitar linked to P.A.)

- ▼ Outriders
- ✡ Singers
- ● Musicians
- ✶ Colourful people dancing and carrying streamers and banners
- □ Banners
- ● Rubbish collectors

Needs between 300-600 people (6 abreast)

When you tell the church about the march, remind them to pray about it together, in housegroups and as individuals. The devil does not like to see the church on the move and may well throw in a few obstacles to frustrate you. A praying people is a mighty weapon against him so enlist this support early and see God working on your behalf. Hold a church prayer meeting during the week before the march and pray at length for the event.

b) When to go

It might be a good idea if you avoided the winter months! The best time is probably a Saturday between April and October. Choose a date and an hour which will suit the public rather than the church. If there happens to be a blizzard or a torrential rainstorm on the day, don't feel guilty about cancelling the event! To go ahead ahead in appalling conditions is to play into the hands of the people who ridicule the church and expect it to do crazy things! You want the bystanders to be amazed at what they see, not to die laughing at a company of well-meaning but sopping wet believers. Go home and fix another date.

c) Where to go

Since you want to go where the people are, your local high street is the most likely place for a procession. The goal is not to take the shortest route but to allow as many people as possible to see you. Because you want the participants to enjoy the walk and not end it on their knees, aim for a march which will last about thirty to forty minutes and walk it through beforehand. If you can, try to avoid steep hills, narrow passageways and streets where major roadworks are proposed! You will need to have a definite starting and finishing point (open spaces at either end of the town, maybe). Everyone must be clear about where to meet and when. You will probably need about half an hour to assemble before the march begins.

Have a look at a map of your town and note down where you could start, continue and finish a praise march.

Start at: ....

Continue along: ....

....

....

....

Finish at: ....

3. Permission

You will need to inform the police of your intention to hold a praise march. Well before the event write a letter starting the date, time and exact route (an enclosed map would be helpful). Mention also that your procession will be well-stewarded by responsible people and request a police escort. Be sure to allow plenty of time for negotiation. The police tend to look favourably on 'religious' marches but they will stop you going along certain roads if this is likely to lead to major disruption. You can apply to the council for a 'road closure order' for the time that you will be in a particular street but it's usually easier to change the route instead. The police may be willing to suggest an alternative plan for you. Be co-operative. That's a witness in itself.

There should be a certain number of stewards, wearing reflective jackets, to every so many people. The police will give you the ratio. Incidentally, do not witness to the policemen while you are walking along. By all means answer any questions they ask, but remember that they are doing a job and must not be hindered in it. It might be a good idea to allocate someone to give out tracts to the policemen after the event. If the whole church knows that this will be part of 'John Smith's' ministry, they can leave it to him and each policeman will receive one tract instead of several!

4. Publicity

a) Clothes

Rather than ask everyone simply to wear bright clothes, why not have a colour theme? This will give a strong sense of unity when everyone is walking along the street. The church will also find it great fun to look out clothing of the appropriate colours beforehand. Try a combination of red, white and blue to start with and, if the praise march is quite long, have the frontrunners in yellow and green. Choose different colour schemes for other marches. You'll be surprised at what comes out of the wardrobe!

Think out four colour combinations and write them here:

1. .... 3. ....

2. .... 4. ....

b) Banners

Banner-making is an excellent housegroup project. Three weeks before the praise march you can decide together on what you want the banner to say and arrange who will do what. A week later you can all begin working on it and you can finish it off on the last housegroup the night before you take it onto the street. You might also like to make some appropriately-coloured streamers. Use bamboo canes and ribbons or crepe paper.

Give four more banner text suggestions.

1. ....

2. ....

3. ....

4. ....

Not all the banners need to be big, but they do have to be clear. The largest ones should be at the front and back. Since tired arms are liable to cause the largest banners to droop, change their 'carriers' frequently during the march. Have at least one banner advertising your fellowship. It should say something like: 'Clarendon Church - Join us at the Odeon - Tomorrow 10.00 a.m.' The banner at the end of the procession could face backwards and read, 'Jesus said, "Follow me!"'

c) Words and Pictures

The literature that you give out should be church-based and include testimonies of people in the church. Each leaflet should include the church's address and a contact phone number. Make sure that the outriders are given a sufficient quantity before the march begins. The balloons that the clown hands to the children could have a text printed on them.

Allocate one person in your fellowship to video the praise march and two to photograph it. The video recording can be shown to the housegroups to encourage (and amuse!) them. The photographs may later be used to advertise the church. Someone should be asked to write a press release after the march and send it to the local newspaper. It should be accompanied by a clear photograph which emphasises the scale of the event. If possible choose a picture which highlights some of the wording on one or more of the banners.

Before the neighbourhood forgets the march conduct two weeks' door to door outreach in the area and ask people what they thought of it.

Chapter Ten
OTHER LARGE EVENTS

When the church is seen to be where the people are, it is bound to attract a positive response. Hold a fun day, get involved in an arts festival or a procession and you have forged links with the world. Draw the general public from there into the church and you can offer them the answer to their real needs.

1. FUN DAY

What is a fun day?
  It's a sort of fete for families.

Where do you hold it?
  On a village green, in a local park or on a school playing field.

When should you have it?
  On an afternoon (2.30-5.00) during the school holidays.

What does everyone do?
  Have fun! (games, competitions ...)

Why do you hold it?
  To put your church 'on the map'.
  To identify with the people and enjoy their company.
  To make contact with those who would like a visit.

To put on a fun day, you will need:

* An overall organiser
* A games/competitions team
* A follow up team

a) The Organiser

The organiser is the one who sets the ball rolling (and tries to keep it going!) He is responsible for the following:

(i) Permission

Before you go into the details of what you're going to do, it's a good idea to find out if you're allowed to do it. Can you simply set up games in the local part or mark out your football pitch on the village green? It's doubtful. The organiser will need to go to the appropriate place to ask for permission. This may be the local authority, the police station or the headmaster's office. He will have to discover exactly what is and what is not permitted and obtain written confirmation.

(ii) Planning

Once you know that you can hold games in a particular location, you can set a date. For a start, make sure that it does not conflict with anything else - either local or international. To choose the same day as the area rugby match or the F.A.Cup Final is not a good idea. The organiser must do a little research on this score.

The organiser will also need to sort out some very practical issues. What about loos? It is not realistic to expect a large number of children to play games for over two hours without providing toilet facilities. (Even the adults might have difficulties!) Make sure there are some toilets that everyone can use and maybe even supply some additional loo rolls on the day.

(iii) Publicity

As the planning gets underway, the organiser will need to consider how to publicise the event. Colourful leaflets and posters which describe the event should be circulated and displayed in the area. Some members of the church could be asked to make a large banner which can be erected on the fun day to advertise both the event and the church. Local newspapers and radio stations should be contacted in advance and asked to mention the occasion. If you choose a date just after the local schools break up, it might be a good idea to take an assembly towards the end of term and to make an announcement then. You might even decide to organise a praise march in the target area a

day or so before the fun day.
What details will you need to circulate to the public?

....

....

....

....

(iv) Participation
The organiser should keep the church in touch with what's happening and share any needs with them. If he can impart enthusiasm, the church will want to be involved and will remember to pray. A few days before the event there should be a specific time of prayer for it.

It is essential to have prayer backing from your church; and to have involvement from them too. Ask people to take the leaflets around the area beforehand. Enlist the help needed to set things up on the morning of the fun day and to take them down afterwards. Encourage helpers to provide plastic cups and large bottles of cold orange squash for the thirsty competitors. It might be a good idea to have someone responsible for a 'queries/lost children' area and someone else commissioned as a childhunter. The idea is that everyone joins in to swell the numbers, to enjoy the event and to get alongside the neighbours.
Where could you fit in?

....

b) Games and Competitions Team

One person in the team will need to be in overall charge. It is the team's job to plan and run all the events on the fun day. This will mean that they have to consider:

(i) The Games and Competitions

Plan to hold a variety of different events to cover a wide age range. Bear in mind the safety angle and try not to select competitions with complicated rules. Remember, the more games you have, the more people you will need to supervise them.

Small children love bouncy castles so see if you can hire one and get permission to put it up. Prepare activities for individuals as well as teams. People can put one another in the stocks and throw soft (or wet) things about. You can have sack or egg and spoon races and hold a treasure hunt. Try a 'Dads and Daughters' piggyback race. A short 'It's a Knockout' competition might go down well too. The main drawback of a long 'It's a Knockout' contest is that it could prohibit latecomers from joining in once the teams have been chosen. You want to encourage involvement, not see people walk away because they are unable to compete.

Write down any other appropriate games that you can think of.

....

....

....

....

(ii) The Equipment

Some of the equipment will be easy to provide but some of the larger items may present a problem. The team will need to find out if things can be borrowed from the local school or, alternatively, where to go to hire them. Will you require P.A. equipment or a loud hailer or neither? A P.A. system will need an electricity source and the loudspeaker will reach only as far as its cable will allow. Try to avoid contravening any by-laws relating to noise level.

Write down what sort of equipment you could need.

scoreboard, footballs, ...

....

....

....

....

....

(iii) The Timetable

Remember, you will need to fill over two hours with games! When you plan your timetable you should find that some of the entertainment can go on all the time (e.g. children on the bouncy castle; throwing things at people in the stocks; coconut shy). Other events will be more competitive. Organise your programme so that there is both free and structured time. You might even like to advertise some specifically-arranged events round the town well in advance (eg 3.30-4.00 Dads versus Boys Football Match - Boys, bring your Dad along! [boys - aged 14 and under])

(iv) The Prizes

All the games will be free but the children will still expect prizes. You will need to decide whether you give out sweets, toys, Bible booklets or a combination of all three. Will you hand the winners the prizes immediately after the competitions or hold a 'grand prizegiving'? If you hold a prizegiving you can take the opportunity to share the gospel and invite everyone to the Sunday night guest service.

c) The Follow-up Team

You have to think up ways of following up a lot of people who are playing games in a field. One way to do this is to arrange to have a photographer at the fun day who can take free portrait-type/family group photos (say, two per family). The parents can leave their names and addresses and someone from the church can call round with the pictures when they have been developed. Any visitors from other parts of the country who just happened to be around for the fun day can be sent their photos along with a tract or an invitation to an evangelical church in their area. You could also arrange to give out cards to people as they leave the fun day. These can state:

> 'We are from ... church and hope you have enjoyed the day. If you are interested in knowing more about us, please contact (name, phone number) or join us one Sunday. Our services are held at (location, time(s)) and we would love to have you with us.'

2. TOWN ARTS FESTIVAL

A Town Arts Festival is a great opportunity for you to share the gospel in drama. Some larger towns hold an annual festival but even if yours does not, you can still give a performance in a large well-populated public park or on the sea-front during the summer.

The drama at a Town Arts Festival should be more a performance than a sketch. The other people who are acting there will be into 'professional' performances so you will need to practise far more than for a quick open air play. Don't be put off either by the professionalism of others or by the amount of rehearsal time involved. God is with you so take the opportunity and use it for His glory.

The salvation message should naturally be the central theme but it can be presented in a variety of ways. You can use either a play from a drama book or you can write your own material. Whatever you do, make it creative, lively, colourful and humourous - and never compromise with the truth. When the drama 'Heartburst' was performed at the Brighton Festival, it had a tremendous impact on people. Actors involved in some of the other plays were impressed by the standard of excellence displayed by the Christians in it. And many of the cast and various church members in the crowd had some superb conversations with those watching. (The script is available from Clarendon Church).

How would you open a conversation with someone next to you who had just seen this drama? Give three different ways.

a) ....

b) ....

c) ....

3. PROCESSIONS

Many towns or villages hold annual carnival processions. They are usually run by the local council or charity group and provide an excellent opportunity for the church to make itself known to other community groups in the town. There is generally a theme for the event and all floats need to be registered and a fee paid. The best float wins a prize so aim to get it!

Make sure that the float is decorated along the lines of the theme - the bigger and brighter, the better. The people on board should be appropriately-dressed. During the procession they should hand out pre-printed balloons and church testimony tracts. If you want to make a little more impact, you could have a small music group walking in front of the float singing lively praise songs.

TO CONCLUDE

Large evangelistic events make the church visible in a way that smaller ones cannot. They also provide a reference point for one to one conversations (What did you think of the float/play? etc). Make the best use of your town's events. Find out what goes on and get involved. Even if you do not see people saved as a direct result, sow the seed. Someone else may have the joy of reaping the harvest.

What events in your town could you turn into evangelistic opportunities?

....

Chapter Eleven
SIGNS AND WONDERS

The world has for a long time had the impression that Christianity is no different from any other religion. 'It's all about what you believe,' people say, What they mean is that it's essentially an intellectual exercise. One individual follows one set of teachings while another prefers something else.

JESUS BUILDS A TEAM

Look into the New Testament and you are not confronted by a Saviour who was just a Teacher. You see a man upon whom the power of God rests. You see someone who demonstrates supernatural qualities: who has amazing wisdom, who knows what people are thinking, who has faith to heal, to work miracles and to cast out demons. Those who encountered Jesus not only heard what He said; they also saw what He did. He confirmed his message by acting on it.
Write out 1 Corinthians 4:20

....

....

When you think about it, Jesus could have come to earth and worked alone. He did need a band of disciples with Him when He taught about the Kingdom, performed the signs of the Kingdom and died to pave our way into the Kingdom. The disciples often seemed to be ignorant of what Jesus was really getting at and were often slow to learn. Why was it, then, that the Master chose the Twelve to be with Him? Surely he was looking for a group of people whom He could train to carry on His ministry when He was no longer physically with them.
Read Luke 9:1,2

What did Jesus give His disciples?

....

What did He expect His disciples to do?

....

....

....

....

What did they do? (9:6)

1. ....

2. ....

3. ....

Jesus later sent seventy-two others to continue this ministry (Luke 10:1-11). Just before He ascended, He commissioned the Eleven to pass on what they had learnt to the disciples they made (Matt 28:19,20). Clearly Jesus expected a gospel of words and works to be proclaimed by His followers. The New Testament book of Acts is an amazing account of what happened when the apostles took Jesus' command at its face value. They preached the gospel and performed signs and wonders among the people.

Do you want the world to see that Christianity is radically different from any other religion? Then don't stop at preaching a salvation message, do the works of the Kingdom as well. When God demonstrates His power in signs and wonders, unbelievers everywhere will marvel at what our God can and does do in the world He loves.

Read the following:

'I tell you something important, many people who have faith in me might do some of the things that I have been doing. They could do some really significant things ...'

Without looking at the Bible reference see if you can correct the above statement.

....

....

....

....

Check your answer in John 14:12

Does what Jesus says here apply to you? YES/NO

Jesus' directions to the disciples were clear: preach and heal. They had heard Him and watched Him. He had told them that He was going away and was giving them the power to carry on His ministry. He expected His disciples to live His life in the world - it included signs and wonders.

1. A Christ-like Team

Jesus wants to live His life through each one of us. Usually we take this to refer to character and general good deeds in a purely 'natural' setting. When we do something 'supernatural', it tends to be at a planned event - a healing service or some sort of large celebration or conference. There is nothing wrong with organised meetings but we must not forget that Jesus' ministry extended beyond the Synagogue. He did not 'switch off' His miracles when He left a traditional place of worship. Indeed, it would seem that He actually performed more signs and wonders in the context of normal day to day living than at any other time.

An open air meeting provides a springboard for good conversations which may lead naturally into signs and wonders. You should, however, not think that you have to wait for an organised event before you step out in the supernatural. Since you belong to a supernatural Kingdom, Jesus expects you to live in a supernatural dimension all the time. This means that you should be ready to be a channel for God's power wherever you are.

I was once walking down the road on my way home from an open air when I passed a lady who was getting out of her car. She was evidently in pain so I stopped, explained that I had just been singing about a God who heals, and asked if I could pray for her. Standing beside the car, I put a hand on her shoulder and prayed. As I did so, the woman felt great warmth in her body and the pain she was experiencing in her side decreased.

Mary, a Christian, was talking to an elderly neighbour who had called in for ten minutes one evening. Just before she left, Florence (not her real name), was complaining about a very painful foot. Mary, who was far from being an expert at asking God to heal people, nevertheless offered to pray and lay hands on the foot. Two evenings later there was a knock at Mary's door. Florence had returned just to say how much better the foot had been since Mary had prayed for it. What prevents you from doing something similar?

....

2. A Believing Team

Rearrange the following into a Biblical verse
Is believes him possible who everything for. (Mark 9:23)

....

....

When Jesus prayed, He believed God for great things. The same mighty power as He had is available to every Christian. This means that we all have the potential for doing all the works that He did. The early disciples were not always successful in what they attempted, but they were obedient to Jesus. Likewise we may not always achieve the results we should like, but we have a command from Jesus to preach and heal and it's up to us to obey it.

As you step forward in faith, be expectant but remember that you are likely to make the most mistakes early on. If you keep this fact in mind, you will safeguard yourself against becoming disheartened when your prayers do not appear to be answered. Keep an ear open for what God is saying and be willing to pray more than once for people if this seems appropriate. In a healing service you might spend a long time asking God to heal someone so don't stop just because you are in a public place. If the individual is still not healed, let him be aware that you care for him even if you do not know all the answers. Give him a church tract before he leaves and assure him of a warm welcome and further help if required.

3. A Compassionate Team

A colleague of mine was once preaching in the open air on Jesus' power to heal the sick. Two women stood in front of him to listen so he stopped speaking and asked, 'Is there anything you would like prayer for?' One of them had arthritis at the base of her spine and allowed him to pray for her. Her condition improved after one session of prayer but as he prayed on, she started to become embarrassed by the curiosity of people who were stopping to watch. The measure of healing she received might have been greater if he had taken her away from the onlookers.

Jesus always treated genuine enquirers as individuals and with

compassion. His healing methods were tailor-made for the people who were seeking His help. Thus He asked someone with a shrivelled hand to 'stand in front of everyone' (Luke 6:8) but took a blind man 'away from the crowd' (Mark 7:33). Sometimes people approached Jesus for healing - for themselves or for others - and on other occasions Jesus took the initiative and went up to them.
Give examples from the Bible of times when:

a) Someone approached Jesus for help

....

b) Jesus approached someone and offered help

....

Be compassionate when you are seeking to use signs and wonders in the open air. It's good to be keen to see God at work in mighty ways, but not at the expense of trampling over an individual's self-respect. Some people are completely at ease if you offer to pray for them in a very public way. Others would like prayer but would prefer a more discreet approach. Be sensitive to individual needs and, as a general rule, tend towards the less public way.

Don't pounce on someone with the offer of healing! Approach him with a tract first of all and progress from there. If you discover that he has a physical need, be sensitive when you ask if he would like you to pray for him and always give him the option of saying 'no'. If he is happy for you to pray with him, you can usually sense if it is appropriate to lay hands on him. If you feel that someone would like you to pray for him but not then and there, you can always say, as one open air member did, 'OK, I'll pray for you as you walk away.'
Write down briefly what you would say to someone who had just told you about a physical need that he has.

....

....

....

Compassion can be a blessing in itself. A Christian who was shopping in a supermarket noticed that a lady had left something behind on the checkout counter. He stopped her near the door and began talking to her. Discovering that she was having trouble with her chest, he offered to pray for her. The woman was so deeply affected by the fact that someone cared that she had to wipe the tears away before she left the shop.

4. A Powerful Team

Jesus' life was characterised by activity and power. Wherever He went He was Himself fulfilling His command to His disciples - preach the gospel and heal the sick. Open airs should not be occasional events, they need to have a consistency about them. If you return to a spot every other week, there is a good chance that you will be able to build up relationships with individuals. This is particularly true of smaller towns and villages.

If you turn up, God will arrange the appointments for you. Before one team left for an open air, one of its members was given a picture of a part of the town close to where the open air was to be held. He had the strong impression that he would see someone there whom he would recognise. Sure enough, he met a family of five whom he knew and who were standing at the exact spot in the vision.

Jot down here the nine gifts of the Spirit mentioned in 1 Corinthians 12:8-10.

....

....

....

....

Since God is sovereign, He can choose to manifest Himself through any of the gifts of the Spirit in a public setting. Having said that, some of the gifts will probably emerge more often in an open air than others. The following are the ones we have found to be most evident:

a) The Word of Wisdom

The teachers of the law and the Pharisees thought they had Jesus cornered. Knowing that adulterers should be stoned, they brought before Jesus a woman who had been caught in the act of adultery. They then reminded Him of the penalty for her sin and waited for His answer.

What did He do at first?

....

How did He reply?

....

....

Check your answers in John 8:6,7

Jesus' reply was carefully weighed and very wise. Sometimes you will find yourself confronted by hecklers or even Christians from other churches who do not like what you are doing. If they try to corner you or put you on the spot, you will need grace and wisdom to know how to deal with them. Send a quick prayer to God to guide you in how you react.

b) The Word of Knowledge

Read John 4:18. What did Jesus know without being told?

....

....

The word of knowledge is a very useful tool in the open air. God tells you something about a person's life that you would otherwise not have known. It usually happens towards the end of the outreach and sometimes during conversation with someone who has been listening.

At one open air a young man received a word of knowledge that there was a lady present whose husband had died recently. He felt God show him who it was and went over and began sharing the gospel with her. The word of knowledge proved accurate and it made the woman very responsive when he told her that God could meet her need.

A young lady called Judy was in the middle of a conversation with

Annette (not her real name) when she received a word of knowledge about Annette's difficult relationship with her parents. When she enquired about this, she discovered that Annette had been thrown out of home and was living with her grandmother. Judy prayed with her about her sense of rejection and hurt and was able to talk about God's power to reconcile.

Al, another Christian, was talking to a lady when he sensed God indicate to him that there was sickness in her family. It turned out that her eighteen year old son was mentally handicapped. Al prayed that God would reveal his love to her in her need and heal the son.

A lady in her twenties was so engrossed in one open air that she didn't notice her small son wander off. When the group learnt what had happened, several of them went off in search of him. The open air leader who had stayed behind with the woman suddenly felt prompted to go into one particular shop. He found the boy there.

c) Faith, Gifts of Healing and Miracles
Give one example from the Bible of each gift

Faith: ....

Healing: ....

Miracles: ....

You may have found it difficult to divorce these gifts from one another. Indeed, when Jesus was confronted by a man who was born blind (John 9:1-9). He exercised faith, provided healing and performed a miracle all at once.

A young man was witnessing to a group of teenagers in the street. They proved to be very antagonistic towards the gospel message and refused his invitation to a meeting. When the Christian began talking about Jesus' power to heal, one of them said, 'I bet your God can't heal my friend's arm.' The friend had been involved in a knife fight. His arm had been slashed and he could not move it very far. The Christian called another believer over and the two of them prayed briefly for him. Much to the amazement of the teenage group, the boy raised his arm high above his head.

Lex wandered into the beer tent at one of the Brighton town festivals. The bands that were playing there were not attracting large crowds - in fact, there were only about five individuals in the audience! Lex met a non-Christian friend in the tent and the two of them asked if they could get onto the stage and play their guitars between acts. They were given ten minutes.

While his friend sat on the stage, Lex stood and sang about Jesus. He had only been singing for about thirty seconds when there was a sudden downpour. To avoid the rain, those outside flocked to the tent and filled it. Lex took full advantage of the miraculous situation. He continued to sing about Jesus and dodged some of the items thrown at him. Only when the ten minutes were up did the rain stop, the sun come out and the people disperse. Lex handed out tracts as they left.

d) Distinguishing Between Spirits

When Jesus was on earth, it was more often the evil spirits who discerned who He was before He indicated His awareness of them! Look up the following and write down how the devil reacted to being in Jesus' presence.

Mark 1:23 ....

Luke 9:42 ....

Mark 3:11 ....

The devil is hostile towards Jesus and therefore towards anyone who follows Him or preaches His Word. Engage in an open air and you become a target for the enemy whom you occasionally need to recognise. An open air preacher sensed that there was something evil behind the abusive comments of a man who was standing directly in front of him. He stopped speaking, put a hand on the man's chest and said firmly, 'Be quiet'. Somewhat startled, the man walked quietly away.

A Christian heard an open air preacher speaking about God's power over the devil. He went up to a few members of the group and began talking to them. Since his girlfriend had left him for someone else, he had lived under a cloud of oppression. The previous night he had been terrorised by jealousy and lust and had a great heaviness resting on his chest. Four of the team members prayed with him, asking God to turn the darkness to light. A pained expression flashed across the man's face. When the group asked the Holy Spirit to come on him he smiled and declared, 'It's gone! it's gone!'

JESUS - STILL BUILDING A TEAM

Jesus said, 'I will build my Church' (Matt 16:18). Today He is building a powerful people, a people who demonstrate supernatural qualities as a way of life. They are receiving His words of wisdom and knowledge and His authority to heal, to work miracles and to cast out demons.

From prison, John the Baptist sent his disciples to find out if Jesus was 'one who was to come' or if he should expect someone else (Matt 11:3). Many people in their worldly prisons want to know if there is a Saviour around now, or if the only help they can ever expect will come via the social services or through a love affair with someone else.
Fill in the gaps to reveal what Jesus replied to John.

'Go back and report to John what you .... and ....: The ....

......................................, the........................... those who ....

.... the ...., the ....

............................., and the .... (vs 4-5)

Jesus gave His early disciples the power to continue His ministry of preaching and healing. The baton now passes to us. The types of people that you have just written down are still with us and they need to see proof that Jesus is not just a good teacher and Christianity not just another religion. The prayer of the early disciples should live with us always:
'Now, Lord ... enable your servants to speak your word with great boldness. Stretch out your hand to heal and perform miraculous signs and wonders through the name of your holy servant Jesus' (Acts 4:29-30).
Let's go and change the world!

LIKE LOOKING INTO A SHOP WINDOW

I don't know why I stopped to watch the open air. I had never shown support to anyone performing on the street before, let alone a small group of Christians. This time, however, curiosity overcame self-consciousness - though characteristically, I remained at a safe distance and well out of earshot!

At that time I was happier than I'd ever been in my life. I'd put behind me years of depression and drugs and now had a place to live; was happy in my job; enjoyed good friends and most of all had a boyfriend I loved very much.

As I watched these young Christians, however, I knew that they were in a different world from mine. They appeared so relaxed and natural, happy just to be themselves. There appeared to be a great bond between them too. Despite the attention they were drawing, they weren't in the least self-conscious, defensive or aggressive - just very normal and enjoying being together and singing.

I became thoughtful, as if looking into a shop window at something I would like but knew I would never have. My world was just different from theirs and nothing could change it. I would always be basically sad and lonely, that's just the way I was. After what I had known before, I couldn't complain.

Being so far away, I certainly didn't expect to be noticed and was rather startled when a girl approached and after a friendly, 'Hello' asked if I was a Christian. I wasn't sure how to reply but when she asked if I had ever invited Jesus into my life I had to say 'No'. I was surprised that she seemed so interested. She then introduced me to another member of the group who told me that Jesus would give me the security I needed. Very taken aback I felt somewhat threatened but knew by then that I was beyond the point of no return.

Although reluctant to go any further, something inside would not let go and I found myself agreeing to visit their coffee bar. There they explained the way of salvation and gently and patiently answered all my questions. For about two weeks I struggled over whether or not to become a Christian. When I finally made up my mind, I phoned one of the team and we arranged to meet very early one morning. We went onto the beach to pray and I gave my life to Jesus.

Claire

FROM INTEREST TO INVOLVEMENT

I was born in Kashmir, India. My parents brought me up as a Muslim but cut me off from the family when I married an English girl. I found a job working for a clothing firm in Sussex and we lived in a flat until she left me in May 1985. I couldn't afford to stay where I was so I moved into a bedsit. My wife divorced me the following February. I had no friends and often found myself wandering alone around the streets and along the seafront.

One Saturday morning I was in Brighton town centre when I saw a group of people singing and dancing. I don't usually stop to watch things that are happening in the street but I was drawn to them. Their music was nice and I was struck by their joy. I stood there and listened for five or ten minutes wondering where they were from. I desperately wanted to find out what was happening and turned to a man and asked him. He told me that they were a group of Christians and invited me to a meeting. I promised him that I would go along.

For the rest of the day and all through the night I couldn't stop thinking about that encounter and about what would happen at the meeting. I was so keen that I arrived almost two hours early! When the service did begin, I was amazed at how relaxed and friendly everyone was. I had been used to a ritualistic religion but here the people were free. I didn't know where I was going but they seemed to have a purpose to life.

As I talked to several members of the church over the next few days I realised that they had the sort of life that I wanted. I became a Christian two weeks after the open air meeting and am now involved in this sort of evangelism myself.

Hassan

HEALED!

'Listen to me. This is proof. I have just been healed!' This lady was testifying at an open air meeting in Hemel Hempstead. About half an hour earlier, she had been standing listening to a group of Christians as they worshipped God. She had cancer then, and a diseased spine which was noticeably bent. When the leader of the group received a word of knowledge that there was someone present with cancer, she immediately stepped forward. A number of Christians prayed with her and after a short time she stood bolt upright, healed!

When she returned with her shopping about thirty minutes later, she asked if she could speak to everyone present. Someone handed her the microphone, someone else took out a video camera and this is what she said:

'Listen to me. This is proof. I have just been healed! In fact ... I'm still a little bit shattered - although I really expected it. I have been extremely ill for twenty years and have never attempted to touch my toes. Now ... I'm going to ... I'm confident enough now to have a go.'

At this point she touched her toes - and everyone involved in the open air became very excited and cheered and praised God. When she stepped down, she was asked to comment further on what had happened. She continued:

'I came to Hemel in pain. I'm going to leave Hemel with no pain. I was told only to get a limited amount of shopping because my husband's not with me and I can't carry much. I've got two bags of shopping. I stood listening to your singers and I knew they were going to help me. I knew it.'

FOR YOUR NOTES

More titles in the

How to...

STUDY SERIES

Effective Evangelism

is a workbook for individuals, groups and church leaders. Beginning with the Biblical teaching on evangelism, it goes on to give practical advice on making contact with non-Christians, giving a testimony, planning a guest service and so on.

Ben Davies is the senior minister of Bracknell Baptist Church, Berkshire. In 1964 the church numbered about 20 people, and today has a congregation of over 500, with 6 full-time staff. Ben also gives pastoral advice to a number of other churches as a member of the *New Frontiers* team. He is a Welshman, and he and his wife Maureen have three teenage children.

Catalogue Number YB 9175 £1.70

Growing up as a Christian

is a book of letters to 9 to 13 year olds, giving practical answers to questions like 'Is pop music wrong?', 'How can I pray?', 'What shall I wear?' and 'Does God really love me?' It encourages young people to see what the Bible has to say about the issues which affect them. This workbook can be used by parents with their children, and by youth leaders as a starter for group discussion.

Roger Day is an editor at Harvestime Publications in Bradford and for many years has been involved in children's clubs and in counselling children. He and his wife Christine have a family of two girls and two adopted boys.

Handling Your Money

is a Bible-based workbook on managing your personal finances. Beginning with the idea of God as giver, the book discusses our attitudes towards wealth, money and possessions. It contains advice on budgeting and avoiding debt, and teaches us how to be abundant givers ourselves. This workbook is suitable for both individual and group use.

John Houghton leads the eldership team at Hailsham Christian Fellowship, Sussex. His wider ministry as a speaker and writer reflects his concern for Christians to face the practical, social and moral implications of the gospel in today's world. John and his wife Janet have three teenage children. His previous books are *Hagbane's Doom, Gublak's Greed* and *Surin's Revenge* (for children), *The Healthy Alternative* and *A Touch of Love.*

Catalogue Number 9176 £1.70

Joining The Church

is a two-part group study course for people considering membership of a local church. The first part consists of four lessons looking at the Bible's teaching on judgment, repentance and faith, baptism in water and baptism in the Spirit. The three lessons in the second part look into what membership of a church involves, covering topics like leadership, housegroups and fellowship.

Richard Haydon-Knowell pastored King's Church, Catford for eighteen years and is now leading Lowestoft Covenant Church in Suffolk. As a member of Terry Virgo's team he has worked with many churches worldwide to help them build according to New Testament teaching. Richard and his wife Sue have four children and the two oldest are now married. Richard's hobbies include photography, painting and the history of art.

Catalogue Number YB 9182 £1.70

Leading a Housegroup

is a training manual covering the many aspects of a housegroup leader's role – from setting goals to leading worship, from teaching Scripture to caring for group members. There are two sessions for the church setting up housegroups for the first time and three chapters for church leaders involved in choosing and supporting housegroup leaders.

Richard Haydon-Knowell pastored King's Church, Catford for eighteen years, during which time the church saw substantial growth. In 1988 he moved with his wife Sue and two of their four children to pastor a new church in Lowestoft. As a member of Terry Virgo's team he has also worked with many churches worldwide to help them build according to New Testament teaching. Richard's hobbies include photography, the history of art and walking.

Learning to Worship

is a devotional workbook for use by both individuals and groups who want, in the author's words, to 'appreciate from the Scriptures this magnificent gem that God has so graciously allowed us to rediscover'. Whether we are worshipping alone or among God's people, this book offers Scriptural insights to help us become the worshippers that God is seeking.

Phil Rogers is the Senior Pastor of New Life Christian Church, South Lee. He is a keyboard player and compiles the yearly songbook for the Downs Bible Week. His own songs include *Who is This?* and *How precious, O Lord.* He is also involved in teaching and training worship leaders. Phil lives in South East London with his wife Sandy and their three sons.

Catalogue Number YB 9179 £1.80

Praying The Lord's Prayer

is a practical workbook for those who want to maintain a consistent and effective prayer life, and can be used by individuals or groups. Taking Jesus' prayer structure as a model, it develops the themes of the fatherhood and names of God, the nature of God's will, reign and kingdom and His gifts and forgiveness in our lives.

Terry Virgo is based at Clarendon Church, Brighton. He also leads the *New Frontiers* team committed to planting and serving churches in the UK and overseas. He is author of *Restoration in the Church* and *Men of Destiny*.

Catalogue Number YB 9177 £1.70